OPEN

SESAME

T0268166

OPEN SEEN

45 Sweet & Savory Recipes
for Tahini & All Things Sesame

SAME

Rachel Belle

Photography by
Charity Burggraaf

SASQUATCH BOOKS
SEATTLE

MORNING MEALS

PARTY SNACKS

MAINS & SIDES

SWEET THINGS

PARTY SNACKS

MORNING MEALS

For my mom

BARBARA

who did not under any circumstances hint that she might like this book dedicated to her

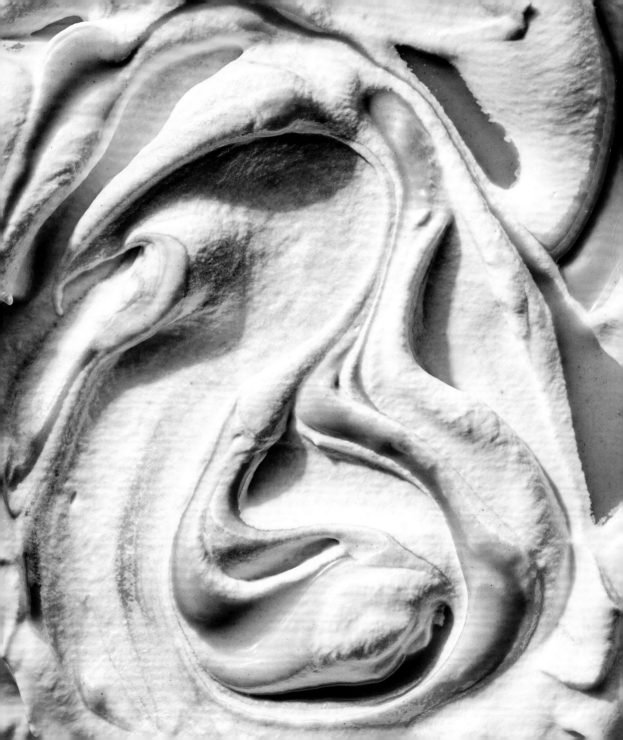

FOREWORD

I bore easily.

Yes, I repeat meals. Yes, I love comfort food. But in the end what really motivates my appetite is finding new things to eat. Rachel Belle is always full of surprises, always full of ideas, constantly challenging the way I look at food.

I met Rachel several years ago when I was a guest on her podcast, *Your Last Meal*. We hit it off immediately, and a handful of months later she flew across the country to cook with me in my Manhattan kitchen.

But when she said she was working on a cookbook, I sighed and hoped for the best. [Author's note: Guffaw!] As a jaded cookbook collector of forty years I was preparing for the worst, and began assembling praiseful phrases that wouldn't let on how bored I was at the prospect of another cookbook trying to reinvent pub food or exaggerate the creature comforts of their childhood food memories.

But then, this slightly insane book about sesame and tahini arrived and I was truly surprised: These are ingredients I haven't cooked with in years, flavors I literally haven't explored since my childhood . . . This was not boring! That's a good sign. Then I started skimming the book: She's very good with words, our Rachel. She says things like *burble* and tells you to cook the strawberries until they are *slumped*. I wouldn't put it past her to stop a total stranger on the street to correct their pronunciation of the word *chhhoumoose*. I began obsessing over the recipes, and everything I knew about the subject of sesame seeds was up for reevaluation. Or, rather, *evaluation*, since I haven't ever really put a lot of thought into the subject.

Having grown up in a Sephardic Jewish home, I ate so many foods that included sesame and tahini. But I took them for granted, never paid much attention to those flavors. When I left my mother's house, I left that cuisine in the dust and went on to explore foods of other worlds.

But as I dog-eared recipe after recipe in this book, my mouth officially watering, I began aching for those flavors again. I immediately ordered two kinds of sesame seeds and a bottle of very good tahini, ready to take part in this flavor revolution. Who among us can resist the sound of Hot Pink Hummus? Gingery Sesame Chicken Soup with Rice Noodles? Tahini Frangipane Apricot Galette?

Those foundational flavors of my childhood that I ran so far away from have been reshaped into shiny, new dishes from the other worlds I dreamed of exploring. And they're anything but boring.

Isaac Mizrahi
PERFORMER, WRITER, AND DESIGNER

INTRODUCTION

Be honest. Have you ever finished an entire jar of tahini? How many times have you bought tahini for, say, a hummus recipe or a salad dressing, used ¼ cup, and then watched it slowly moonwalk to the back of the refrigerator, unsure of what to do with the rest? *slowly raises hand*

Here at *Open Sesame*, we believe in No Tahini Left Behind!

Like a little black dress, tahini can seamlessly transition from day to night, from savory to sweet, from the Middle East to the Midwest, with a healthy drizzle baked into your morning granola (page 13), poured over Pita Chip Nachos (page 29) in the form of creamy Tahini Feta Queso (page 33), and whipped into desserts like Chocolate Miso Whoopie Pies with Tahini Cream (page 111). Tahini: it's not just for hummus! But I'll show you how to make a fantastic version of that too.

This book is a celebration of sesame in its many forms: the earthy warmth of sesame oil shimmering on the surface of a noodle soup, the toasty crunch of a sesame seed–crusted schnitzel, and the deep, dark nuttiness of black sesame paste blended with dates, banana, and milk.

But the origin story of this book is rooted in a Tahini Epiphany™.

Growing up in the 1980s with an Israeli-raised dad, my family ate a fair amount of *chhhoumoose*. That's how we pronounce *hummus*—the Hebrew way, with the signature guttural, phlegm-clearing roll in the back of the throat (she's one page into her cookbook and she's already said *phlegm*?). Chhhhhouuumooooose! This was before "hummus" was a household name in the United States, before you could buy seven varieties (Pumpkin spice hummus!

Chocolate hummus!) at Trader Joe's. This was before we'd ever *heard* of Trader Joe's!

Hummus is simple: a creamy puree of chickpeas, tahini, lemon, garlic, ice water, and salt. But every time I made a batch in my own kitchen, it never tasted quite right. I tried everything: tirelessly peeling the papery skins off every single garbanzo bean, soaking dried beans in baking soda–spiked water. The hummus I ordered in restaurants, or bought from the supermarket, wasn't any better.

Several years ago after an event I attended at the Stroum Jewish Community Center in Mercer Island, Washington, we were treated to a Middle Eastern nosh. I half-heartedly scooped an obligatory blob of paprika-dusted hummus onto my tiny plate, dragged a wedge of pita through it, took a bite, and, reader, I immediately lost my mind.

"Who made this hummus!?" I squawked, zipping around the room, interrupting groups of kibbitzing strangers with my broken-record question. This was it! The flavor I'd been chasing for over a decade! I was given the phone number of the caterer, an Israeli man my father's age, and the next weekend I was standing in Eli Lahav's kitchen watching him make chhhoumoose.

He cranked open a giant can of chickpeas from a restaurant supply store, glugged an ungodly amount of tahini into the food processor, and after a single taste, it became clear: delicious hummus relies completely on delicious tahini! I needed better tahini and lots of it.

Not long after, I interviewed the chef-owner of Seattle's Aviv Hummus Bar for my podcast, *Your Last Meal.* Aviv serves life-changing hummus, the best I've tasted outside of Israel, and when I asked him what makes his hummus so special, he confirmed: it's the tahini. He wouldn't share which brand he uses, but he offered me a clue: he only buys tahini from Israel.

A shipment of Har Bracha Tahini later, I was ready to try again. I blitzed all the usual suspects in my blender, dipped a spoon in for a taste, and stood

in my kitchen in disbelief: I finally re-created that nostalgic flavor memory in my own kitchen.

Hummus means a lot to a lot of people. Historians believe it originated in Syria and Egypt, but the dish has been a steadfast staple in all Arabic cultures for centuries. The cultural history of hummus in the Middle East is a major point of contention, which I discuss more on page 39.

But this book is so much more than hummus, or even Middle Eastern cuisine. Tahini is your plant-based ticket to creaminess, an understudy for peanut butter when allergies are at play, and its mild nuttiness was destined for desserts.

Sesame is one of the most ancient ingredients, eaten by humans for thousands of years. Grown in Asia, Africa, and South America and exported around the world, it finds its way into the kitchens of so many cultures.

In *Open Sesame*, we'll explore some familiar Asian and Middle Eastern applications for sesame, get creative with takes on Mexican and Indian dishes, and sprinkle sesame on some American classics.

Not All Tahini Is Created Equal!

Tahini is made from a single ingredient: toasted sesame seeds. That's it! Just roasty-toasty, teeny-tiny sesame seeds ground down to a silky, beige, peanut-buttery paste. No salt. No added oil. Just sesame.

But each brand of tahini can taste quite different depending on where the sesame seeds were grown, what variety they are, if they're hulled (creamy and mild) or unhulled (gritty and bitter), how deeply they're roasted, and how many months (or years!) that jar has been languishing on the store shelf. Unfortunately, you rarely see any of that information on the label.

But choosing a good tahini is important! A bitter tahini can muck up a dish (especially in hummus and sauces where the tahini is front and center) and trick you into thinking the recipe is to blame.

So how *do* you choose the best tahini? Allow me to tahini-splain to you:

* Buy tahini made from white Humera sesame seeds. Grown in the northwest corner of Ethiopia, this variety is considered the world's best. All Israeli tahini (or *tahina*) is made from Humera seeds, and when I researched where my favorite brands of tahini were made, coincidentally they were *all* from Israel. Turkey, Jordan, and Saudi Arabia are also importers of Humera sesame, but it's unclear if all their tahini is made with it.

* Shop at a Middle Eastern or international market. If you love to cook, you probably love taking field trips to a variety of grocery stores. While mainstream supermarkets *can* carry good tahini, you'll find a larger variety at a specialty store. Choose a couple bottles of tahini from different countries, and see what you like! If you don't have a market in your area, order popular brands online (my suggestions follow).

* Check the expiration date! This might sound obvious, but I recently came home with one jar of expired tahini and another that had been bottled more than a year before (it wasn't technically expired, but definitely not fresh). Next time I'll take my own advice!

* Make sure the tahini is easy to stir. If you're struggling with claylike clumps or a thick layer of murky oil, it's probably past its prime. If the tahini is clumpy but still tastes good, scrape it into a food processor and blitz it back to silky smoothness.

* Consider buying squeeze bottles of tahini. While it doesn't affect flavor, having the ability to shake a bottle (no stirring!) and squirt tahini directly onto my waffles (recipe on page 17) or into a tablespoon has me reaching for the tahini far more often.

Tahini Tips

* Tahini + cold water sitting in a tree! The best way to thin tahini into a sauce or a dressing is with cold water. Tahini tends to seize up when blended, but cold water smooths it right out. Add a little at a time until you get the viscosity you desire.

* Mix your tahini well before each use!

* Store open jars of tahini in a cool, dark place or in the fridge.

* If you're left with a small amount of tahini at the bottom of a jar, make a dressing or sauce by adding your other ingredients directly into the jar and shaking vigorously.

General Notes

* All recipes in this book were tested with Diamond Crystal Kosher Salt. If using Morton Salt, use half the amount.

* All recipes were tested with extra-virgin olive oil.

* All recipes call for tahini made with 100 percent sesame seeds, no salt, no additives.

* Many recipes call for untoasted sesame seeds, since they will be toasted during the cooking process. If a recipe calls for toasted seeds, you can

MY FAVORITE TAHINIS

Har Bracha

Soom ← Their dark chocolate tahini with sea salt is swoonworthy!

Mighty Sesame

Haddar by Baracke

Seed + Mill

* All recipes call for tahini made with 100 percent sesame seeds, no salt, no additives.

* Many recipes call for untoasted sesame seeds, since they will be toasted during the cooking process. If a recipe calls for toasted seeds, you can add your raw sesame to a dry pan over medium heat and gently toast until golden, watching and stirring constantly so they don't burn.

* All recipes using sesame oil call for toasted sesame oil.

* If your sesame seeds have been around awhile, give them a sniff. You'll be able to tell if they've gone off.

I encourage you to make environmentally friendly choices whenever you can! Instead of marinating chicken in a plastic ziplock bag, try a lidded container. Dry off chickpeas with a dish towel instead of paper towels. If buying small amounts of bulk spices, bring your own containers and have the tare recorded by a grocery store clerk.

CONGEE

WITH SESAME SOY MUSHROOMS

AND

JAMMY KOREAN MARINATED EGGS
(MAYAK GYERAN)

This congee is like one of those high school makeover movies where the nerd (leftover rice) takes off her glasses (slowly simmers in chicken broth), shakes out her ponytail (add sesame oil, ginger, garlic), and poof! She's crowned homecoming queen (best breakfast in the book)! Starting with cooked rice cuts the cooking time in half, making congee a manageable morning meal. *Mayak gyeran* translates to "drug eggs" in Korean because they're so addictively delicious. This recipe makes more eggs than you need, but you'll be happy to have leftovers. Bursting with umami, these gooey eggs can be added to noodle soups, salads, or a bowl of warm steamed rice drizzled with the spicy sesame soy marinade. The eggs need to marinate for at least six hours, so start them the night before.

(CONTINUED)→

Makes 2 bowls for 2 hungry people

FOR THE EGGS:

6 large eggs

½ cup soy sauce or tamari

½ cup water

2 large garlic cloves, minced

1 tablespoon sesame oil

1 tablespoon unseasoned rice vinegar

1 teaspoon honey

1 small jalapeño, seeded, thinly sliced
  or minced

FOR THE CONGEE:

2 packed cups cooked white rice
  (not basmati; see Note)

4½ cups chicken broth (I use
  5 teaspoons of chicken Better
  Than Bouillon plus water)

1 (2-inch) knob of ginger, peeled and
  minced or grated

2 large garlic cloves, sliced thin

½ to ¾ teaspoon salt (you may need
  more if using lightly flavored boxed
  chicken broth)

1 tablespoon salted butter

1 tablespoon plus ½ teaspoon sesame
  oil, divided

½ pound button mushrooms, trimmed,
  wiped clean with a damp dish towel,
  and quartered

1 tablespoon soy sauce

1 tablespoon mirin

1 to 2 green onions, white and green
  parts thinly sliced on a bias

Sesame seeds, for garnish

Chili oil, for serving (optional)

NOTE: One cup of uncooked rice makes enough for two cups of cooked rice.

1 To make the eggs, bring a pot of water to a rolling boil and carefully lower in the eggs. Set a timer for 7 minutes for jammy yolks or 8 minutes for fudgy yolks. (Adding eggs to hot water makes them easier to peel, and you can control the cook time.) Immediately transfer the boiled eggs to a bowl of ice water.

2   While the eggs cool, whisk the soy sauce, water, garlic, sesame oil, rice vinegar, honey, and jalapeño in a tall container (like a plastic deli container) with a lid.

3   Peel the eggs, fully submerge them in the marinade, and pop them in the fridge for at least 6 hours or overnight. If they're not totally submerged, turn them over in the marinade every couple of hours.

4   When the eggs are ready, start the congee.

5   In a medium-large pot, bring the cooked rice, chicken broth, ginger, and garlic to a boil, then immediately turn the heat down to a low burble. Stir the congee often so it doesn't stick to the pot. Cook for about 30 minutes until it's a loose porridge, with the texture of risotto, adding more water as needed. Season with salt to taste.

6   While the rice cooks, heat a large pan over medium and melt the butter with 1 tablespoon of the sesame oil. Add the mushrooms and sauté for a few minutes, until all of the flat sides of the mushrooms are golden, then add the soy sauce and mirin. Sear the mushrooms on all sides until they're deeply brown, about 3–5 minutes.

7   Divide the congee into two shallow bowls. Drizzle each with ¼ teaspoon of sesame oil, scatter the green onions, and top with the mushrooms.

8   Cut 2 eggs in half lengthwise and add to the bowls. Sprinkle the mushrooms and eggs with sesame seeds. Serve with chili oil, more sesame oil, and the egg marinade, if desired.

TIP: Remove remaining eggs after they're done marinating and store separately in the fridge. The leftover egg marinade will keep in your fridge for a week or two. You can marinate more hard-boiled eggs in it or spoon it over rice, cooked vegetables, and proteins.

ROASTED STRAWBERRY TOAST WITH GOAT CHEESE AND TAHINI

I know that we're just getting to know each other, and I should probably hold your hand a bit longer. But . . . you're on your own, dude! The problem is bread. Specifically, slices of bread. I have no idea how large yours are! And I won't ask you to bring a measuring tape to the supermarket to measure the width of artisan loaves, no matter how much I'd like to see the looks you'd get. So I can't very well tell you how much goat cheese to spread or how much tahini to drizzle! But here's the thing: I trust you. I really do! Schmear on the amount of goat cheese that feels right to you. Top your toast with a jaunty little zigzag of tahini. Make it rain basil! Look at you: you're free! My friend and recipe tester Genevieve describes this toast as a "delicious, fancy PB&J." The roasted strawberries are also a tasty topping for oatmeal, plain yogurt, pancakes, waffles, and vanilla ice cream.

 CONTINUED →

Makes 4 large slices of toast or 8 small slices

1 pound fresh strawberries, hulled and
   sliced into quarters
2 tablespoons honey
2 teaspoons balsamic glaze or
   balsamic vinegar
A few cranks of freshly ground pepper
Pinch of kosher salt

Thick sliced bread from a crusty loaf
   (I like sourdough)
4-ounce tube plain goat cheese
Flaky salt, for sprinkling
A handful of fresh basil leaves, thinly
   cut into strips or a chiffonade
Tahini, for drizzling

1 Preheat the oven to 425 degrees F.

2 Add the strawberries, honey, balsamic, pepper, and kosher salt to an 8-by-
8-inch baking pan. (You don't want them spread out in a large pan.) Roast for
about 30 minutes, until the strawberries are slumped and very soft and juicy.
Break them up a bit with a wooden spoon.

3 Toast as many slices of bread as you'd like. Generously schmear one side of each
toast with goat cheese, all the way to the edges. Spoon on some strawberries
and their juices, sprinkle with flaky salt and basil, and drizzle with tahini.

ALEPPO-SPICED TAHINI YOGURT

WITH

BURST TOMATOES AND SESAME FRIED EGG

Sweet, jammy burst tomatoes make every dish pop, including my version of *çılbır*, or Turkish yogurt eggs. A lifelong fan of dinner for breakfast (as a kid, I ordered spaghetti at a Denny's at 8 a.m. on a family vacation and would set my alarm to beat my sister to leftover Chinese food), this is my kind of savory Sunday brunch. Bread is optional but oh-so tasty dragged through the tangy tahini yogurt with a little bit of everything piled on top. Oh, and don't fret about the heaping spoonful of Aleppo chili; it's fruity and mild, more flavor than fire, mellowed even further by the cold, creamy yogurt.

Makes 2 servings

1 tablespoon olive oil

8 ounces cherry tomatoes,
   such as Sungold

½ teaspoon salt, plus more
   for seasoning

½ cup plain full-fat Greek yogurt

3 tablespoons tahini

1 medium or large garlic clove, grated

2 tablespoons freshly squeezed
   lemon juice

1¼ teaspoon ground Aleppo chili

1 to 2 teaspoons toasted sesame oil

2 large eggs

Everything Bagel Seasoning (page 48,
   or store-bought) for sprinkling

Freshly ground black pepper

6 cucumber slices, ½ inch thick

Crusty bread, warm flatbread, or toast,
   for serving (optional)

CONTINUED→

1 Heat the olive oil over medium high in a pan with a lid, then add the tomatoes. Cover, turn the heat down to medium or medium low, and stir every few minutes, adding a small splash of water if they get too dry or sticky. When the tomatoes are very soft and slumped, 15 to 20 minutes, press them with a wooden spoon to release their juices. Season with a pinch of salt.

2 While the tomatoes cook, mix the yogurt, tahini, garlic, lemon juice, Aleppo chili, and ½ teaspoon salt in a small bowl.

3 Divide the yogurt between two plates, spreading a wide, thick bed, and top each with half the tomatoes and their juices.

4 Wipe out the pan you cooked the tomatoes in. Heat the pan over medium, add the sesame oil, and fry the eggs until the edges are crispy and the centers are gooey, flipping once so the yolk is enclosed.

5 Slide an egg on top of each yogurt bed and sprinkle the finished dish with everything bagel seasoning and a few cranks of pepper. If your bagel seasoning is salt-free, season the eggs with a pinch of salt. Pierce the yolks and let them mingle with the tahini yogurt.

6 Serve with chunky cucumber slices and hunks of crusty bread for dipping.

TROPICAL TAHINI PINEAPPLE SMOOTHIE

I am not a culinary creature of habit . . . except when it comes to this smoothie! Day after day, week after week, year after year, I stand before my whirling blender, under a frizzy cloud of morning hurricane hair, still awed and energized by its glorious green hue. Are there handfuls of spinach in this smoothie? Yes! Is there a healthy chunk of cucumber? Yes! Will you taste either of them? Strangely, no! It gives tropical sweetness, balanced by the earthiness of tahini, and finishes with the gloriously smug feeling that you've consumed the daily recommended number of vegetables before 9 a.m.

Makes two 16-ounce smoothies

1 medium banana

½ cup plain Greek yogurt
  (any fat percentage)

⅓ cup cold water or coconut milk, plus
  more as needed

1 (2-inch) chunk of cucumber, quartered

1½ ounces (a big handful or a heaping,
  packed cup) fresh spinach

¼ cup tahini

1¼ heaping cups frozen pineapple,
  plus more to taste

¼ teaspoon salt

• Toss all the ingredients into a blender, preferably a high-speed model like a Vitamix, in the order listed for easiest blending. Blend until completely smooth. If you have a standard blender, it might take a few minutes. Add a bit more cold water if it's too thick and needs help blending. If it's not sweet enough for your taste, add a bit more frozen pineapple.

TIP: This smoothie stores well in a sealed container in the fridge overnight. I always make the whole batch, drink one, and pop the other into a sealed mason jar in the fridge for tomorrow's easy grab-and-go breakfast, sipped on my way to work or the mountains.

CHONKY
TAHINI MAPLE GRANOLA
WITH PISTACHIOS AND COCONUT

Packed into a mason jar with a handwritten masking-tape label, this nubbly, clustery granola makes the perfect gift. It's been sent off on camper-van road trips, tucked into my mom's suitcase before she returns home, and delivered to doorsteps during the holidays. It's only lightly sweetened, bordering on savory, which makes it an excellent topping for Greek honey yogurt, but I prefer it under milk with lots of freshly sliced or freeze-dried strawberries. Once the recipe becomes your own, feel free to swap in any nuts you have in your pantry—slivered almonds or roughly chopped pecans. Store prominently in a jar on your countertop to give your kitchen that *easy-breezy* "Oh, I make my own granola" vibe.

Makes about 8 cups

¾ cup real maple syrup

½ cup tahini

3 tablespoons coconut oil

2 teaspoons vanilla extract

1 teaspoon cinnamon

1 teaspoon salt

½ teaspoon nutmeg

3 cups old-fashioned oats (not instant)

1 cup shelled pistachios

1 cup pepitas

¼ cup toasted sesame seeds

½ cup unsweetened coconut flakes/chips

Freeze-dried strawberries or fresh berries, for serving (optional)

Yogurt or milk, for serving (optional)

CONTINUED →

1 Preheat the oven to 325 degrees F and line a 13-by-18-inch baking sheet with parchment paper.

2 Combine the maple syrup, tahini, coconut oil, vanilla, cinnamon, salt, and nutmeg in a glass mixing bowl. Heat in the microwave, covered, and stir every 45 seconds, or gently heat in a small saucepan on the stove over low, stirring until melted and no lumps remain.

3 In a large bowl, combine the oats, pistachios, and seeds. With a rubber spatula, scrape the wet ingredients into the oat mixture and stir until completely and evenly incorporated.

4 Spread evenly onto the prepared baking sheet and bake for 25 minutes.

5 Pull the sheet out of the oven and evenly scatter the coconut flakes on top. Return to the oven and continue baking until golden, 5 to 10 minutes, checking frequently to ensure the coconut doesn't burn. Do not mix.

6 Let the granola cool completely—this is how it gets crunchy! This could take about an hour. Crumble into chunks or whatever size makes you happy. Scatter freeze-dried strawberries on top or add them when serving. Serve with yogurt or milk with fresh berries on top, or serve as-is as a snack. Store in a sealed container for up to 2 months.

SESAME-CRUSTED WAFFLES
WITH TAHINI AND MAPLE

Biting into a toasted sesame bagel slathered with melted butter, I had a thought: This would be really good as a waffle. Both sides of these waffles are encrusted with black and golden sesame seeds, and cornstarch is added to the batter to ensure maximum crispness. Want more sesame? You've come to the right book. We are gathered here today to celebrate the delicious marriage of tahini and maple syrup! You can also make a savory waffle by nixing the sugar and vanilla and mixing shredded cheddar and green onions into the batter before topping with tahini, avocado, a fried egg, and hot sauce.

Makes 4 square waffles

1 cup all-purpose flour

2 teaspoons baking powder

2 teaspoons cornstarch

1 tablespoon sugar

¾ cup whole milk

4 tablespoons salted butter, melted
(if you use unsalted, add ½ teaspoon
salt to the dry ingredients)

1 teaspoon vanilla extract

1 large egg

Nonstick cooking spray, for the
waffle iron

½ cup untoasted sesame seeds, plus
more as needed (a mix of black and
white or just white)

Tahini, for serving

Real maple syrup, for serving

CONTINUED →

1   Heat a waffle iron.

2   In a large bowl, mix the flour, baking powder, cornstarch, and sugar.

3   In a medium bowl, mix the milk, melted butter, and vanilla. Add the egg and whisk it together for about a minute.

4   Add the wet ingredients into the dry and mix until just incorporated.

5   Spray the waffle iron with nonstick cooking spray and generously sprinkle in enough sesame seeds to completely cover the grooves in the waffle maker. Add the batter and sprinkle a single layer of sesame seeds on top.

6   Cook until golden brown and crisp. When the waffle iron's indicator light comes on, check the waffles and leave them in longer if they're still soft or pale. I often leave them in twice or three times as long and they've never burned!

7   Serve with plenty of tahini and maple syrup. Leftover waffles can be stored in an airtight container in the fridge for several days or in the freezer for a couple months. Reheat in a toaster or 350-degree F oven until crisp.

TIP: If making several batches of waffles, heat the oven to 250 degrees F and transfer waffles from the iron to the oven to stay warm and crisp while you finish up the batter.

CRUNCHY FURIKAKE SNACK MIX

A few years ago, I made a custom snack mix for a friend heading out on a road trip, loaded with all his salty, crunchy favorites. When I started daydreaming about *my* perfect mix, this Crunchy Furikake Snack Mix with Japanese rice crackers and savory sesame sticks was born. It wasn't until I searched "Furikake Chex Mix" online that I learned it's a well-established sweet and salty Hawaiian favorite, made with corn syrup, Post Honeycomb cereal, and Bugles. Just so there's no confusion, my version is different! Perfect for those with more of a salt molar than a sweet tooth.

Makes 12 cups

3½ cups Rice Chex

3½ cups Corn Chex

2 cups kaki no tane Japanese rice crackers (commonly found at Asian markets or online)

1 cup sesame sticks

1 cup Goldfish crackers

1 cup pretzels (a small shape like mini twists or sticks)

1 stick (½ cup) salted butter, cut into smaller chunks

2 tablespoons soy sauce

1 teaspoon sugar

1 teaspoon Lawry's Seasoned Salt

1 teaspoon garlic powder

1 batch Simple Sesame Furikake (page 25), or store bought

CONTINUED →

1 Preheat the oven to 250 degrees F and position two racks toward the center of the oven.

2 In a large bowl, mix the cereals, rice crackers, sesame sticks, Goldfish, and pretzels.

3 In a small microwavable bowl or in a small pot on the stove over medium-low heat, gently melt the butter before adding the soy sauce, sugar, Lawry's, and garlic powder, stirring to combine. If using the microwave, cover the bowl with a dish towel and microwave on high in 30-second increments until melted.

4 Mix the furikake into the butter mixture and pour half of it over the snack mix, stirring well. Fold in the remaining butter mixture, making sure every last crispy snack is coated.

5 Spread the snack mix across two 13-by-18-inch sheet pans (if you have smaller pans, you'll need more than two so it toasts evenly) and place them on the middle racks. Bake for an hour, stirring every 20 minutes, until golden and crunchy. Let the mix cool for 10 minutes before serving to ensure maximum crunch. If storing, make sure it's cooled completely. It tastes best the first 2 to 3 days, but lasts up to 2 weeks in a sealed container in a cool, dry place.

Simple Sesame Furikake

Furikake is a crunchy, salty Japanese condiment most commonly sprinkled on steamed rice. There are dozens of varieties that include dehydrated salmon flakes, *umeboshi* (pickled plum), shredded shiso leaves, wasabi, little bits of dehydrated egg, and almost all of the blends prominently feature sesame seeds. This is the most classic version, my go-to mix-in for onigiri. The way furikake turns ordinary steamed rice into a briny, umami treat makes me wonder if it's merely coincidence that it looks like party confetti.

Makes ½ cup

4 sheets toasted nori

¼ cup toasted sesame seeds

1½ teaspoons sugar

1 teaspoon salt

- Accordion fold a sheet of nori into seven strips. Stack the strips and, using kitchen shears or clean scissors, cut them into four long strips. Hold the pile of strips together over a bowl and snip into super thin confetti-size flakes. Repeat with the other three sheets of nori. In a small jar or container, add the nori confetti, sesame seeds, sugar, and salt. Shake well before using. In an airtight container, this should keep for at least a month.

FALAFEL-SPICED TAHINI DEVILED EGGS
WITH CRISPY CHICKPEAS

Deviled eggs are a head-to-head competitor with pigs in a blanket for First Snack to Get Eaten at a potluck, picnic, or party, and this creative take on the classic—heady with the familiar flavors of falafel—brings something new to the table: crunch! If you're a mayo hater who normally steers clear, these dudes are made with tart and creamy Greek yogurt and tahini. I believe they're called deviled eggs because tediously peeling off the shells is a task commanded by the devil himself. But if you follow this boiling method (painstakingly tested by recipe developer J. Kenji López-Alt), they should peel right off like a nice, long, satisfying strip of wallpaper. Oh, and I don't want to brag, but the crispy chickpea garnish is so good, I caught my cat with her head in the bowl, happily crunch, crunch, crunching away.

Makes 12 deviled eggs

FOR THE CRISPY CHICKPEAS:

1 (15.5–ounce) can chickpeas, rinsed and well–drained

1 tablespoon olive oil

½ teaspoon ground cumin

½ teaspoon ground coriander

½ teaspoon garlic powder

½ teaspoon salt

Freshly ground black pepper

FOR THE EGGS:

6 large eggs

¼ cup plus 1 tablespoon plain Greek yogurt (any fat percentage)

¼ cup tahini

1 tablespoon plus 1 teaspoon freshly squeezed lemon juice

2 medium cloves garlic, grated or finely minced

2 tablespoons very finely minced fresh parsley, plus more for garnish

1½ teaspoons ground cumin

1½ teaspoons ground coriander

1 teaspoon salt

Paprika (smoked or regular), for garnish (optional)

CONTINUED →

1 Preheat the oven to 425 degrees F and put a medium-large pot of water over high heat to boil.

2 Lay a clean dish towel on a baking sheet and pour the chickpeas on one half. Fold the other half of the towel on top and roll the chickpeas around until they're dry.

3 Remove the towel but keep the chickpeas on the baking sheet and coat them thoroughly with the olive oil, spices, salt, and pepper. Roast on the middle rack until crisp but not rock hard, 25 to 35 minutes. Let them cool on the counter.

4 When the water is at a rolling boil, carefully lower in the eggs and set a timer for 15 minutes. Prepare an ice water bath and when the eggs are done, transfer them to the ice water until cool.

5 Peel the eggs, cut each in half, and scoop their yolks into a bowl. Add the yogurt, tahini, lemon juice, garlic, parsley, cumin, coriander, and salt and mix until creamy. If the yolks are dry or stodgy, add a bit more yogurt and tahini.

6 Pipe or spoon the yolk mixture back into the egg whites and garnish with a shake of paprika, a sprinkle of parsley, and the crispy chickpeas; I like four or five on each deviled egg.

7 If you have leftover chickpeas, throw them into a salad or eat them as a snack within a couple days.

PITA CHIP NACHOS

WITH TAHINI FETA QUESO AND CHICKEN SHAWARMA

Tangy, crunchy, creamy, and zesty, thanks to salty feta and loads of bold spices, this Middle Eastern take on nachos hits all the same pleasure centers as its Mexican cousin and makes a fun party snack or a snacky dinner. The components of these nachos can also be mixed, matched, and morphed into other meals: you could stuff the chicken, tahini queso, and salsa into a pita; serve it over a bowl of grains; or pare it down to just the pita chips and queso. But I don't recommend skipping the chips; dusted with sumac and toasty sesame seeds, they're so addictively delicious I like to make a double batch so I have something to snack on after the nachos are long gone. When you're buying pita, make sure they have pockets, as opposed to the thicker, pillowy flatbread sometimes labeled Greek pita. Chips and queso can be made a day ahead and stored in sealed containers in the pantry and fridge, respectively.

 CONTINUED →

Makes 4 to 6 servings

FOR THE CHICKEN:

2 tablespoons olive oil

2 tablespoons freshly squeezed
   lemon juice

¾ teaspoon salt

2 teaspoons smoked paprika

1 teaspoon Aleppo chili

½ teaspoon ground cumin

½ teaspoon ground turmeric

½ teaspoon garlic powder

½ teaspoon ground sumac

¼ teaspoon ground cinnamon

¼ teaspoon ground allspice

Several cranks of freshly ground
   black pepper

1 pound boneless, skinless
   chicken thighs

FOR THE CHIPS:

4 pita pockets, white or whole wheat,
   cut into chip–size triangles

3 tablespoons olive oil

1 teaspoon ground sumac

½ teaspoon salt

1 to 2 tablespoons untoasted
   sesame seeds

Tahini Feta Queso (page 33)

FOR THE SALSA:

1 pint cherry tomatoes, such as
   Sungold, halved

Half an English cucumber
   (6 inches), quartered and cut
   into bite–size cubes

1 teaspoon olive oil

Salt

Quick Pickled Pink Onions (page 34),
   for serving

1 To make the chicken, in a medium-size storage container, whisk the olive oil,
lemon juice, salt, and all the spices. Add the chicken and make sure it's fully coated
on all sides. Snap on the lid and marinate in the fridge for at least 4 hours, ideally 8
or overnight.

2 When the chicken is marinated, transfer to a baking sheet or glass baking pan.

CONTINUED →

3   To make the chips, preheat the oven to 350 degrees F. While it preheats, separate each pita triangle into two, cutting or carefully tearing along the seam so they are one layer each. On a baking sheet, toss the pita with the olive oil, sumac, and salt until evenly coated.

4   Arrange the pita in a single layer and sprinkle sesame seeds on top. Pop the pita chips and the chicken into the oven. (The chicken can also be seared on the stovetop or grilled if you want crispy bits and char.)

5   Bake the chips until crisp, 10 to 15 minutes, flipping halfway through so both sides are golden brown. Bake the chicken for 20 to 22 minutes, until juicy and cooked through. Let the chicken rest for 10 minutes and chop into bite-size pieces.

6   While the chicken and chips bake, make the queso and set aside.

7   To make the salsa, in a small bowl, mix the tomatoes and cucumbers with the olive oil and a pinch of salt to taste.

8   On the pan the pita was baked on, or on a platter, spread out the pita chips and drizzle over the queso. Top with the chopped chicken, salsa, and pickled onions, mindful that each chip gets a little bit of everything.

TIP: When a recipe calls for lots of spices I don't have in my pantry or ones I don't regularly use, I shop at a grocery store with a bulk spice section and only buy the exact amounts I need.

Tahini Feta Queso

As many a therapist has wisely advised, unmet expectations can lead to disappointment. So I'm going to let you know exactly what to expect! This isn't a warm queso. But trust me, it's so tasty you won't even notice. Tangy and creamy, it's a lovely contrast to warm dishes like Crushed Potatoes with Tahini Feta Queso and Olive Tapenade (page 67) or Pita Chip Nachos with Tahini Feta Queso and Chicken Shawarma (page 29).

Makes ¾ cup

3 ounces feta

¼ cup tahini

2 to 4 tablespoons cold water

2 tablespoons freshly squeezed lime juice

1 small or medium jalapeño, seeded and roughly chopped

- In a small food processor, blend the feta, tahini, 2 tablespoons of cold water, lime juice, and jalapeño until smooth and pourable, like a creamy salad dressing. If it's too thick, blend in another tablespoon of cold water and repeat as needed.

CONTINUED →

Quick Pickled Pink Onions

Growing up with two parents of Eastern European Jewish descent, I ate pickles like other kids ate ketchup. My mom always served her meatloaf and mashed potatoes alongside a ceramic dish of pickley things—dill pickles, marinated artichoke hearts, my dad's garage-cured olives, surreptitiously swiped from a tree in our dentist office parking lot. Only when my school friends visited for dinner was I told this was not a "normal" combination. But lots of cultures use pickled veg to cut through rich, earthy flavors. These quick pickled onions will perk up everything from nachos and tacos to sandwiches, burgers, salads, and scrambled eggs.

Makes one 16-ounce jar

1 large red onion
½ cup unseasoned rice vinegar
¼ cup sugar
1 tablespoon salt

1½ cups hot water (that has been heated on the stove, but not quite boiling)

1 Cut the onion in half and, flat sides down, cut into thin slices.

2 Pour the rice vinegar, sugar, and salt into a 16-ounce jar. Pour the hot water into the jar. Tighten the lid and shake vigorously, until the sugar and salt dissolve into the liquid. Pack the onions into the jar and pop into the fridge to cool. The onions are ready when they're tinted pink and cool, at least an hour. Pickled onions will keep in the fridge in a tightly lidded container for a month.

ETHEREALLY CREAMY
ISRAELI-STYLE HUMMUS

Here she is, my pride and joy. I must warn you, there's no going back after this. Snobby symptoms include losing your ability to enjoy grocery store hummus, pronouncing *hummus* with a Hebrew accent (chhhoumoose!), and ordering large quantities of Israeli tahini online. Ask your doctor if Ethereally Creamy Israeli-Style Hummus is right for you. Many hummus recipes call for a few tablespoons of tahini, but the secret to *fantastic* hummus is a nice big pour of high-quality tahini (see page xxi for my favorite brands) and, ideally, a good pummeling in a high-speed blender until it's as smooth as cake frosting. If you don't have a high-speed blender, run your food processor or blender for at least five minutes to smooth out *every* last speck of chickpea. Many folks insist on cooking dried chickpeas, but as long as you're using delicious tahini, I find that canned is perfectly fine. Don't skip the finishing drizzle of olive oil; the grassy, peppery notes bring it all together.

Makes about 2 cups

2 medium garlic cloves

¼ cup (from 1 to 2 lemons) freshly squeezed lemon juice, plus more to taste

1½ teaspoons salt, plus more to taste

½ cup Israeli tahini

Cold water, as needed

1 (15.5-ounce) can chickpeas, drained and rinsed

Good quality extra-virgin olive oil, for finishing

Paprika, for garnish (optional)

Flaky salt, for garnish (optional)

CONTINUED →

1   In a food processor or blender (ideally a high-speed blender like a Vitamix), blend the garlic, lemon juice, and salt and let sit for 10 minutes to mellow the garlic.

2   Add the tahini and blend until smooth. If the tahini seizes up, add a teaspoon of cold water and repeat as needed until it's pourable.

3   Add the chickpeas and blend until extremely creamy. If it seizes up, add a little cold water and repeat as needed. If you're using a food processor or regular blender, blend for several minutes until the hummus is the texture of frosting: thick but fluffy, no chunks or grainy bits remaining. Taste and season with more lemon juice or salt as needed.

4   Spread the hummus into a shallow bowl and, using the back of a spoon, press down lightly while slowly turning the bowl to create a swoopy valley. Drizzle a generous amount of olive oil into the valley and garnish with a scattering of paprika and flaky salt. Serve with olives and the best pita or flatbread you can find. (Some Middle Eastern restaurants bake theirs fresh daily and sell it to-go.) The hummus will keep refrigerated in a tightly lidded container for up to 5 days.

A NOTE ON HUMMUS

Hummus may be a simple dish, but the humble puree of chickpeas and sesame paste carries a complex historical and political weight.

Hummus has found itself at the heart of an emotional debate between Palestinians and Israelis. Though hummus is often referred to as the unofficial national dish of Israel, Palestinians view it as a cherished part of their heritage and express concern over the appropriation of their cuisine. When Arab-conceived dishes like hummus, falafel, and tabbouleh are categorized as Israeli food, many Palestinians experience it as a reflection of the ongoing occupation, and even erasure, of Palestinian culture.

Hummus has been eaten in Palestine, Egypt, Turkey, Lebanon, Syria, and Jordan for many hundreds of years. When Palestine was divided to make Israel a state in 1947, the tiny country was flooded with Jewish refugees from around the world. These immigrants sunk their teeth into the local ingredients and adopted many ubiquitous Middle Eastern dishes as their own.

My dad was just a baby when he and my paternal grandparents, both Holocaust survivors, immigrated to Israel in 1948, and my lifelong love of hummus is baked into my personal relationship with Israeli food and culture. I have strong childhood memories of visiting my grandma in Israel, my family tucked into a café courtyard, watching rapt as a couple of women pulled freshly puffed, flame-flecked pita from the maw of a woodfire oven. Decades later, I still remember the revelation of that warm, pillowy bread, its chewy crumb nothing like the dry, cardboard pita we bought from the supermarket at home. We tore off hunks to drag through warm plates of creamy hummus, baba ghanoush, and other Middle Eastern salads and dips.

I call my recipe "Israeli-style" hummus simply because it's what I know best. My preference for Israeli tahini is based solely on the familiar flavor of the buttery, crushed Humera sesame seeds.

Although it can be tough to separate politics from a cuisine that has transcended from food into a symbol of culture, history, and identity, my personal taste is based solely on flavor and memory. Through my hummus recipes, I aim to celebrate the rich history of a dish that is loved by so many cultures.

GOLDEN HUMMUS

Just like your mom secretly has a favorite child, I have a favorite hummus recipe. Don't tell the others but . . . it's this one! Admittedly, I added the golden beet and turmeric purely for aesthetics, imagining a few showstopping, colorful dips for a party spread. But when I lowered my spoon into the blender for a taste, I was instantly smitten by the warm and earthy flavors. Serve alongside the Hot Pink Hummus (page 44) and a plate of vibrant-green cut vegetables (for dipping!) to create a psychedelic, rainbow snackscape. I love it as a dip with fresh pita or Rustic Sesame Lavash Crackers (page 45), but it's also delicious on a veggie sandwich or schmeared inside a falafel or shawarma pita sandwich.

Makes about 2 cups

2 medium garlic cloves

⅓ cup (from 2 to 3 lemons) freshly
squeezed lemon juice, plus more
to taste

1½ teaspoons salt

1 medium golden beet, peeled and cut
into medium chunks

½ cup tahini (see page xxi for my
favorite brands)

1 teaspoon turmeric powder

Cold water, as needed

1 (15.5-ounce) can chickpeas, drained
and rinsed

Good quality extra-virgin olive oil
for finishing

Flaky salt, for garnish

1   In a food processor or blender (ideally a high-speed one like a Vitamix), blend the
    garlic, lemon juice, and salt and let sit for 10 minutes so the garlic can mellow.

2   Meanwhile, place the beet chunks in a microwave safe bowl, cover, and microwave
    on high for 2 to 5 minutes until totally tender. Or, on the stovetop, steam until
    tender, about 10 to 12 minutes. Let the beets cool to room temperature.

CONTINUED →

3 Add the tahini, beets, and turmeric to the garlic mixture and blend until smooth. If the tahini seizes up, add a teaspoon of cold water at a time until it flows again.

4 Add the chickpeas and blend until ethereally smooth and creamy, adding a little more cold water as needed if it seizes up. If you're using a food processor or regular blender, blend for several minutes until the hummus is the texture of frosting: thick but fluffy, no chunks or grainy bits remaining. Taste and season with more lemon juice or salt as needed.

5 Spread the hummus in a shallow bowl, and using the back of a spoon, press down lightly while turning the bowl to create a swoopy valley. Drizzle a generous amount of olive oil into the valley and garnish the whole thing with flaky salt. The hummus will keep refrigerated in a tightly lidded container for up to 5 days.

Hot Pink Hummus

Makes about 2 cups

Look at this color! Magenta, hot pink, fuchsia! All thanks to a single, humble beet. Follow the directions for Golden Hummus (page 43) but swap out the golden beet with a red beet and omit the turmeric. Serve on its own or alongside the Golden Hummus for a dramatic and colorful snack spread.

RUSTIC SESAME LAVASH CRACKERS

These seedy crackers are *so* easy to make, they're the perfect unintimidating project for a Nervous Baker™. There's no yeast, no waiting for dough to rise, and you probably have most, if not all, of the ingredients lurking in your pantry. In places like Armenia, Iran, and Azerbaijan, lavash is the daily (flat)bread, eaten with most meals. To make them shatteringly crisp, like we do here, the dough is rolled out paper-thin. Stack these up next to a bowl of hummus or on a charcuterie board and let the "You *made* these crackers?" wash over you. Their size is choose-your-own-adventure: I like the drama of a giant cracker, but smaller, individual-sized ones can be more practical for a crowd.

Makes 4 large crackers or 16 smaller ones

1 cup all-purpose flour
¼ teaspoon kosher salt
½ cup water, plus more as needed
2 tablespoons plus 8 teaspoons
   olive oil, divided

8 teaspoons sesame seeds (a mix of
   black and white looks nice, but one
   color is perfectly fine)
2 teaspoons smoked paprika
½ teaspoon garlic powder
½ teaspoon onion powder
Scant teaspoon flaky salt

1 Preheat the oven to 375 degrees F and line two baking sheets with parchment paper.

2 In a medium bowl, mix the flour and salt, then add ½ cup water and 2 tablespoons olive oil. This can also be done in a stand mixer. Mix until shaggy, adding more water if dry, a teaspoon at a time. Transfer the dough to a lightly floured surface and knead until it forms a smooth ball, about 10 to 15 pushes.

CONTINUED →

3 Cut the dough into four equal pieces and cover three of the chunks with a dish towel while you roll out the first cracker. Lightly flour your work surface and, using a rolling pin or the pasta attachment on a stand mixer, roll out the dough until extremely thin, about 1 centimeter thick, 13 inches long, and 7 to 9 inches in its widest spot.

4 Transfer to a baking sheet and cover with a kitchen towel. Roll out the rest of the crackers, transferring them to the baking sheets and covering as you go.

5 Using a fork, prick each piece of dough about ten times. This ensures the cracker will stay flat while baking, but some bubbles are lovely! Drizzle 2 teaspoons of olive oil over each piece of dough, and use your fingers to coat the entire surface.

6 Mix the sesame seeds, smoked paprika, garlic powder, onion powder, and flaky salt in a small bowl and sprinkle evenly across each piece of dough, pressing the seeds into the dough with your fingers.

7 Now you get to choose the size of your crackers! Either leave them whole, for a dramatic presentation, or cut each one into four pieces.

8 Pop both sheets onto the middle rack of the oven for 10 to 13 minutes, until the edges are golden and everything is crisp. Immediately transfer to a cooling rack. Serve immediately or store in a sealed container for about a week.

NOTE: You can use store-bought everything bagel seasoning instead of the suggested topping, but many brands are quite salty, so I recommend making a homemade blend, like the Everything Bagel Seasoning on page 48.

CONTINUED →

Everything Bagel Seasoning

For decades, we sunk our teeth into everything bagels, completely unaware that a versatile seasoning blend was literally right under our noses. Like many modern couples, bagels and everything bagel seasoning are no longer monogamous, and this open relationship has delicious benefits. Use it to jazz up sliced avocado or eggs, like in the Aleppo-Spiced Tahini Yogurt with Burst Tomatoes and Sesame Fried Egg recipe (page 9), to season salmon (Everything Including the Bagel Salad on page 57), or mix it into panko when breading chicken for schnitzel in the Challah Chicken Schnitzel "Shabbat Sandwiches" (page 89). I find some of the store-bought mixes too salty, so this homemade version allows you to use as much, or as little, salt as you like. I prefer to use flaky salt; the bigger flakes cling to the seeds and alliums instead of dropping to the bottom of the jar.

Makes a heaping ½ cup

3 tablespoons toasted white sesame seeds

2 tablespoons dried minced garlic

2 tablespoons dried minced onion

1 tablespoon black sesame seeds

1 tablespoon poppy seeds

1 teaspoon flaky salt, such as Maldon, plus more to taste

TIP: If you don't keep these ingredients in your pantry, it is far more affordable to buy exactly as much dried garlic, dried onion, and poppy seeds as you need in the bulk spice section of your grocery store.

1 In a dry pan, toast the dried garlic and onion, stirring with a spatula every 10 to 20 seconds until it takes on a uniform toasted color, the shade of a light-brown paper lunch sack. Be careful not to let it get too dark or it will turn bitter.

2 Transfer to a small jar or container and add the sesame seeds, poppy seeds, and flaky salt. Shake the jar and let it cool completely before putting the lid on.

3 If you want an extra-toasty mix, toast everything but the salt in a dry pan, add it to the jar, and then mix in the salt. Add more salt to taste.

4 Shake the jar before using.

TAHINI, SOUR CREAM, AND CARAMELIZED ONION DIP

When I was a kid, sour cream and onion dip was only "for company." My mom would tear open a packet of Laura Scudder's Toasted Onion dip mix, stir it into a tub of sour cream, serve it to her friends playing mahjong at the dining room table, and, no matter how much I begged, I wasn't allowed to dip a single chip! The only reason Child Protective Services didn't get involved is because I was given free rein to scrape the nearly empty bowl the next morning. My passion for sour cream and onion dip has never cooled, so I came up with this homemade version, with big plops of tahini and a tangle of copper-colored caramelized onions. The flavors mingle and intensify with time, so make it a day ahead if you can. Serve with potato chips and/or raw veggies like cucumber spears, bell pepper strips, jicama rods, and carrot sticks.

Makes about 1½ cups

3 tablespoons olive oil

1½ pounds (2 medium) yellow onions, halved and sliced thin

1½ teaspoons salt, divided

1 (8-ounce) container sour cream (about 1 cup)

¼ cup plus 1 tablespoon tahini

2 teaspoons freshly squeezed lemon juice

1 teaspoon soy sauce

1 teaspoon onion powder

½ teaspoon garlic powder

A scattering of finely chopped chives, for garnish (optional)

CONTINUED →

1 Heat the oil in a large pan over medium heat and add the onions. Cook for 5 to 8 minutes, lowering the heat if they start to crisp. Turn the heat down to medium low or low, put the lid on, and stir every few minutes so they don't stick or burn. You want the onions soft, jammy, sticky, and caramel colored, but not crispy. This will take between 40 minutes and an hour. If the pan gets too dry, deglaze with a splash of water.

2 When the onions are caramelized, mix in ½ teaspoon salt. Adding the salt at the end keeps the onions moist while they cook! You can caramelize the onions a day before making the dip.

3 Transfer the onions to a cutting board and, when cool, chop them finely. In a medium bowl, mix the sour cream, tahini, lemon juice, soy sauce, onion powder, garlic powder, and the remaining 1 teaspoon salt. Mix in the onions.

4 In a small food processor or blender, blend half the dip, add it back into the bowl, and stir well. Let the dip rest in the fridge for at least an hour, preferably 4 to 24 hours. The longer it sits, the better it gets!

5 If you want your dip to look cute (for company!!!), garnish with the chives! Store leftovers in a sealed container for up to 5 days.

ONIGIRI

WITH

HOMEMADE FURIKAKE

Japan is a culinary wonderland, but real ones know the most cravable bite costs less than 200 yen (less than $2) and is a ubiquitous snack at every Japanese convenient store. Onigiri is soft, chewy rice pressed into a triangle shape and wrapped in a crisp kimono of seaweed just before eating. A textural experience, the snap of the salty seaweed giving way to pillowy rice is what makes them so addictively delicious. Onigiri is often stuffed with a dollop of tuna mayo (my favorite), kombu (savory seasoned kelp), a nug of salmon, or umeboshi (pickled plum), but when I make them at home, I skip the fillings and simply flavor the rice with lots of furikake. A favorite hiking snack, onigiri can be thrown into my pack without needing refrigeration. On that note: do not refrigerate, unless you're a fan of dry rice! Onigiri are traditionally wrapped in plain, toasted nori, but Korean sesame seaweed snacks, lush with sesame oil, make them an even tastier treat.

Makes 4 onigiri

1 cup short-grain Japanese rice

½ cup Simple Sesame Furikake (page 25) or your favorite variety of store-bought, divided, plus more to taste

1 teaspoon salt, plus more to taste

1 packet sesame seaweed snacks (see Note)

(CONTINUED)→

1 Cook the rice according to package directions. Fluff the rice. Shake up the furikake so it's well-mixed just before use. While the rice is still hot, mix in ¼ cup of the furikake, ideally with a rice paddle. Scoop the furikake from its container with a spoon, making sure you get the salt and sugar that settled on the bottom. Add in the remaining ¼ cup of the furikake and the salt and mix again. You want the furikake completely distributed. Season with more salt and/or furikake to taste.

2 Scoop out ½ cup of rice and, with damp hands, form into a ball, flatten slightly, and use your hands to shape it into a triangle, or pack the rice inside an onigiri mold.

3 If you're saving the onigiri for later, tightly wrap each one in plastic wrap but don't refrigerate. When ready to eat, stick a sesame seaweed snack to the front and the back of the onigiri and enjoy the contrast of the soft rice and crispy seaweed. Onigiri are best eaten the day they are made.

NOTE: Sesame-flavored seaweed snacks are widely available at Asian markets and some traditional supermarkets. Costco makes an excellent Kirkland brand snack. Onigiri molds can be found at some Japanese markets and online.

·EVERYTHING INCLUDING· THE BAGEL SALAD·

I love a Ladies Who Lunch workday salad. But if a salad is going to be the whole meal, there better be some buttery chunks of avocado, a scattering of crispy tortilla strips, some *buried treasure* lurking beneath the lettuce, like a toy at the bottom of the Cracker Jack box. In this deconstructed bagel-and-lox salad, craggy hunks of crunchy, seedy bagel make for delicious salad booty, giving day-old bagels new purpose. A silky fillet of seared salmon stands in for lox, goat cheese is a stunt double for cream cheese, and a lemony tahini dressing ties it all together.

CONTINUED →

Makes 2 bowls

FOR THE SALAD:

1 sesame seed or everything bagel,
  torn into crouton-size pieces
1 tablespoon plus 2 teaspoons olive or
  avocado oil
3 teaspoons Everything Bagel
  Seasoning (page 48), divided
1 (8-ounce) salmon fillet (or a pound if
  you want a heartier meal), cut in half
Salt
2 heads Little Gem lettuce,
  roughly chopped

1 (4-inch) chunk of English
  cucumber, sliced
Handful of cherry tomatoes, such as
  Sungold, halved (only use if
  in season or looking good!)
1 ounce goat cheese, crumbled
2 teaspoons capers
Quick Pickled Pink Onions
  (page 34; optional)
Lemon wedges, for serving

FOR THE DRESSING:

⅓ cup olive oil
Zest of 1 lemon
¼ cup lemon juice (from 1 to 2 freshly
  squeezed lemons), plus a few lemon
  wedges for serving
3 tablespoons tahini
2 tablespoons minced chives
2 tablespoons minced shallot

1 tablespoon cold water, plus more
  as needed
2 teaspoons Dijon mustard
1 teaspoon honey
½ teaspoon salt
A couple twists of freshly ground
  black pepper

1 Preheat the oven to 375 degrees F. Place the torn bagel on a baking sheet, drizzle with 1 tablespoon of the olive oil, and sprinkle with about a teaspoon of everything bagel seasoning. Toss to coat and press the bagel chunks into the seeds scattered on the pan. Bake until toasty and golden brown, crunchy but not hard, flipping halfway through, 8 to 12 minutes. Remove from the oven and set aside.

2 To make the dressing, in a small food processor or with an immersion blender, blend all of the dressing ingredients until emulsified. If it's too thick, add another teaspoon of cold water and blend, repeating as needed.

3 Pat the salmon skin dry and season lightly with salt. Sprinkle the top of the fillet with 1 to 2 teaspoons of everything bagel seasoning (more if you're cooking a 1-pound fillet), making sure it's evenly coated and gently pressing it in so it sticks. If your blend doesn't have salt, season the flesh of the salmon with another sprinkle of salt.

4 Heat 2 teaspoons of olive oil in a cast-iron pan or skillet over medium high and add the salmon skin side down. After a minute, turn the heat down to medium. Every piece of salmon has a different thickness, so cook time will vary and you'll want to keep an eye on it. When the sides of the fillet look 75 percent cooked (around 6 minutes), flip the salmon and cook for another 30 seconds to a minute. The thickest part of the salmon should be 120 to 125 degrees F. Transfer to a plate skin side up so the precious crispy skin doesn't get soggy.

5 Arrange the lettuce in two wide bowls, add the cucumbers and tomatoes, and toss with the dressing. You may not want all of it, so mix in a little at a time until it's perfect for you. Top with the goat cheese, croutons, capers, salmon, and pickled red onions. Serve with lemon wedges and shoulder pads if you're a lady who lunches.

BEET SALAD

WITH

GARLICKY TAHINI ᴬᴺᴰ MINT GREMOLATA

Once upon a time, before kale salads were king, there was another ubiquitous salad on every menu in America. Her name was Beets, Candied Nuts, and Goat Cheese, and everybody wanted to order her. Everybody except me! It was those dang nuts, which were always too sweet, too sticky, too big, hard, and clunky. But earthy beets were meant to be paired with crumbles of creamy, salty cheese! This salad gets its crunch from tiny toasted sunflower seeds; its brightness from a minty take on gremolata (inspired by a recipe in Eden Grinshpan's glorious cookbook *Eating Out Loud*); and its creaminess from feta and tahini dressing. To make the dish more of a rib-sticking main or to zhuzh up your leftovers, serve it over a chewy cooked grain like wheatberries, farro, or brown rice.

Makes 4 to 6 servings as a side

FOR THE SALAD:

1½ pounds red or golden beets, peeled, quartered, and cut into 1½-inch wedges

¼ cup crumbled feta, plus more for topping

1 batch Garlicky Tahini Sauce (page 63), divided

FOR THE GREMOLATA:

3 tablespoons toasted sunflower seeds

3 tablespoons thinly sliced (chiffonade) fresh mint

3 tablespoons olive oil

1 tablespoon lemon zest

¼ teaspoon salt

CONTINUED →

1   In a medium pot fitted with a steamer basket, add several inches of water. Add the beets to the basket. Over medium-high heat, steam the beets until tender, about 15 minutes. They're done when easily pierced with a knife. Transfer to a serving bowl or plate to cool on the counter or in the fridge.

2   To make the gremolata, in a small bowl, mix the sunflower seeds, mint, olive oil, lemon zest, and salt.

3   When the beets are completely cool, toss with the feta, drizzle half the tahini sauce over the top, spoon on the gremolata, and serve the rest of the tahini sauce on the side. Toss the salad just before eating, coating every beet with sauce, and feel free to add more cheese.

Garlicky Tahini Sauce

Please meet the workhorse of this book! This easy tahini sauce can be drizzled on any roasted vegetable or into a pita cradling falafel or shawarma. It can be thinned out and used as a salad dressing; you can dip your fries into it, cast spells with it, fingerpaint with it, and on and on and on! Several recipes in the book call for this tahini sauce, so I expect this page will soon be splattered and stained, the highest compliment for any cookbook.

Makes ¾ cup

⅓ cup tahini

¼ cup cold water, plus more
  as needed

3 tablespoons freshly squeezed
  lemon juice

1 medium garlic clove, grated or
  finely minced

¼ teaspoon salt

- Whisk the tahini, cold water, lemon juice, garlic, and salt in a bowl until very smooth, or blend in a small food processor. If the tahini seizes up or the sauce is too thick, add another teaspoon of cold water and repeat as needed. Store in an airtight container, in the fridge, for up to a week.

ROASTED KABOCHA SQUASH
WITH
TANGY MISO–TAHINI DRIZZLE

Kabocha squash is so custardy, so velvety and luscious, I often eat it steamed and naked (the squash, not me!), tender skin and all, standing over the billowing pot. But you deserve a sprinkle of salt. Heck, you deserve a sauce! Miso, soy, and sesame is a classic Japanese combination, a bright and salty contrast to the mellow squash. Serve as a simple, satisfying meal over steamed rice or bulk up your rice bowl with sliced avocado, roasted chicken thighs, or salmon. The sauce is also delicious over asparagus, Japanese sweet potatoes, cauliflower, or broccolini.

Makes 4 to 6 servings as a side

1 (2– to 3–pound) kabocha squash, scrubbed (they're big; you might only need half)

2 tablespoons toasted sesame oil, or more for larger squash

Salt

2 green onions, white and green parts thinly sliced

1 tablespoon sesame seeds

FOR THE TAHINI-MISO SAUCE:

¼ cup tahini

2 tablespoons warm water, plus more as needed

2 tablespoons yellow miso paste

1½ tablespoons honey

1½ tablespoons freshly squeezed lime juice

1 tablespoon soy sauce

1 tablespoon unseasoned rice vinegar

2 teaspoons sesame oil

1 small garlic clove, finely chopped

CONTINUED →

1 Preheat the oven to 415 degrees F (425 is soooo 2023!).

2 Cut the squash in half, scoop out the seeds, and carefully cut out the stem. Slice each half into 1–inch wedges like you'd cut up a cantaloupe. Keep the skin on; it's tender and edible!

3 On a large baking sheet, coat the squash in sesame oil and season lightly with salt. Add more oil as needed; you want it well slicked so it doesn't dry out. Spread out the wedges so they're not touching (you might need two sheets) and roast on the middle rack, flipping the squash halfway through. Roast until a knife can easily pierce through, 25 to 30 minutes.

4 While the squash roasts, make the sauce. Blend all ingredients in a small food processor or whisk them together in a small bowl, adding more warm water as needed if it's too thick. You want a glossy, pourable sauce.

5 Transfer the squash to a serving platter and drizzle generously with the miso-tahini sauce. Scatter the green onions and sesame seeds on top and serve.

CRUSHED POTATOES

WITH TAHINI FETA QUESO AND OLIVE TAPENADE

Yes, this dish is delicious, blah blah blah, but arguably the *best* part of the recipe is the task of crushing tiny boiled potatoes under the weight of a drinking glass. I'm not sure if this technically qualifies as ASMR, but there is a subtle snap and a *very* satisfying *feeling* as the little potatoes burst out of their skins. After the flattened potatoes are pan-fried, they're topped with a creamy tahini feta sauce and buttery Castelvetrano olives, which add a lovely zing to the humble, blank canvas of a crispy potato.

Makes 4 to 6 servings as a side and more as an appetizer

FOR THE POTATOES:

1 to 1½ pounds baby potatoes
(gold, red, or a mix)

Salt

Olive oil, for cooking

1 batch Tahini Feta Queso (page 33)

FOR THE OLIVE TAPENADE:

8 pitted Castelvetrano olives, finely
chopped (see Note)

1 medium clove garlic, grated or
finely minced

3 tablespoons finely chopped
fresh parsley

3 tablespoons olive oil

2 teaspoons red wine vinegar

Pinch of salt

A handful of chopped fresh mint
leaves, for garnish (optional)

CONTINUED →

1   To make the potatoes, boil them in salted water until just fork tender, 10 to 15 minutes. Be careful not to overcook so they don't fall apart.

2   Meanwhile, make the sauces. To make the olive tapenade, mix all the ingredients except for the mint in a small bowl.

3   Drain the potatoes and transfer to a cutting board to slightly cool for a couple minutes. Using a glass or mug (or the bottom of a cat food can like my recipe tester did?!), press down on each potato until just crushed and flat, but not falling apart.

4   Heat a ½ inch of olive oil in a large skillet over medium high and add the potatoes in a single layer, working in batches and adding more oil as needed. Sprinkle both sides lightly with salt. Cook until brown and crispy, about 5 minutes on each side. Turn down the heat if they're threatening to burn.

5   Transfer the potatoes to a serving platter, drizzle generously with tahini feta queso, and spoon the olive tapenade on top. Sprinkle with mint leaves.

NOTE: Castelvetrano olives can be found in jars, at the olive bar, or in plastic clamshells in the deli section at most supermarkets. Double-check they don't have pits!

GINGERY SESAME CHICKEN SOUP
WITH RICE NOODLES

This cozy chicken soup, seasoned with splashes of soy, sesame oil, and a big ol' hunk of ginger, is exactly what I want on a cool, rainy day. Or while stuck in a camper-van on the Trans-Canada Highway for three hours due to a sinkhole. If I can make "sinkhole soup" in a van on the freeway, you can certainly pull it off in your home kitchen! This isn't a pho recipe, but I live in Seattle, where there are more pho shops than Starbucks, so I instinctively finished this rice noodle soup with a scattering of fresh herbs and a big squeeze of lime. Don't skip the lime; it magically awakens all the other flavors, like a late-night rendition of Neil Diamond's "Sweet Caroline" at a karaoke bar.

Makes 4 generous servings

3 tablespoons toasted sesame oil, plus more for serving

½ small yellow onion, sliced thin

1 (4–inch) chunk of ginger, peeled and grated

1 large garlic clove, sliced

¼ teaspoon salt, plus more to taste

8 cups (2 quarts) flavorful chicken broth (I like Better Than Bouillon)

1.5 to 2 pounds chicken legs or 1 pound boneless, skinless chicken thighs

7 to 8 ounces medium–width rice noodles (about half a standard package)

1½ to 2 tablespoons soy sauce (you'll need more if your chicken broth isn't very flavorful)

10 ounces (3 to 4) baby bok choy, sliced lengthwise into quarters or eighths

1½ limes, cut into quarters, divided

2 green onions, white and green parts, sliced thin

A handful of chopped fresh cilantro, for garnish

A handful of thinly sliced fresh Thai basil leaves, for garnish

Chili crisp, chili oil, or sriracha, for serving (optional)

 CONTINUED →

1   In a large soup pot, heat the sesame oil over medium heat.

2   Add the onions and sauté for a few minutes until soft. Add the ginger, garlic, and salt and stir constantly to prevent sticking. Pour in the broth and use a wooden spoon to scrape the bits off the bottom of the pot.

3   Bring the soup up to a boil. Add the chicken and turn the heat down to low. Partially cover the pot, letting the soup gently simmer for about a half hour, until the chicken is cooked through.

4   Meanwhile, in a medium pot filled with water, cook the rice noodles according to package instructions. Drain and rinse off the starch with warm water. Set aside.

5   When the chicken is cooked through, transfer to a plate. When cool enough to handle, remove the skin and bones (if using legs) and shred the meat.

6   With the broth on a low simmer, add 1½ tablespoons soy sauce and the baby bok choy and cook until the veg is just tender, 5 to 7 minutes.

7   Turn off the heat, stir the shredded chicken back into the pot, and drizzle the soup with a bit of sesame oil and the juice of half a lime. Taste and add a bit more soy sauce, sesame oil, and a dash of salt if the broth needs more flavor.

8   Divide the rice noodles between four bowls and ladle the soup on top. Garnish each bowl with green onions, cilantro, and basil and serve with the remaining lime wedges and chili crisp.

RAINBOW FARRO BOWLS
WITH HERBY TAHINI SAUCE

I'm a sucker for a beautiful, colorful, nourishing grain bowl crowded with vegetables. But if humble cabbage and radish elicit nothing more than a disinterested shrug, clearly you haven't had them roasted! Radishes surrender their signature sharpness, slumping into mild, creamy orbs, and caramelized purple cabbage gets sweet and tender with frizzled, crispy edges. This dish is a master class in multitasking: while the vegetables roast, you'll be boiling eggs, caramelizing leeks, cooking chewy farro, and blending an herby tahini sauce. But it's so worth it! This recipe makes enough for four, but I often make a batch for myself to eat for lunch throughout the week.

Makes 4 servings

1½ cups farro

1½ to 2 pounds purple cabbage, cut in half, core removed, and sliced into ½-inch-thick chunks

2 bunches (about 20) radishes, trimmed and halved

4 tablespoons plus 1 teaspoon olive oil, divided

1¼ teaspoons salt, divided, plus more for sprinkling and to taste

1 large bunch (½ pound) broccolini

1 very large leek or 2 smaller leeks, white and light-green parts rinsed and sliced

12 baby potatoes, halved

4 large eggs

1 teaspoon salted butter

Hot sauce, for serving (I like it with chili crisp!)

Quick Pickled Pink Onions (page 34; optional), for serving

FOR THE HERBY TAHINI SAUCE:

⅓ cup tahini

¼ cup plus 2 tablespoons cold water

¼ cup fresh parsley leaves

20 fresh mint leaves

20 fresh basil leaves

1 tablespoon lemon zest

3 tablespoons freshly squeezed lemon juice, plus more to taste

¾ teaspoon salt, plus more to taste

1 medium or large garlic clove (to your taste)

A few cranks of freshly ground black pepper

NOTE: The tahini sauce and eggs can be made a day in advance.

 CONTINUED→

1 Preheat the oven to 425 degrees F.

2 Cook farro according to package directions.

3 In a large bowl, toss the cabbage and radishes with 1 tablespoon plus 1 teaspoon olive oil and 1 teaspoon salt. Arrange in a single layer on your largest baking sheet. In another large bowl, coat the broccolini with 1 tablespoon olive oil and ¼ teaspoon salt and arrange on a second baking sheet.

4 Roast the broccolini until the stems are just tender and the florets are crisp, about 20 minutes, turning them every 5 minutes. Roast the radishes and cabbage until the radishes are soft and the cabbage is crisp and caramelized around the edges, about 30 minutes, turning everything every 5 minutes. If both pans don't fit on the middle rack, rotate them halfway through.

5 Meanwhile, heat 2 tablespoons of olive oil in a large pan over medium heat and add the leeks. Turn the heat down to low, gently sautéing and stirring often until jammy and caramelized, about 30 minutes. Add a splash of water anytime the pan gets dry and the leeks threaten to crisp.

6 Meanwhile, boil the potatoes in a large pot of salted water until tender. When the water is rapidly boiling, gently lower the eggs into the potato pot. Boil for 7 minutes for jammy yolks or 8 minutes for fudgier yolks. Transfer the eggs to an ice bath and, once cooled, peel and slice in half lengthwise. Sprinkle each half with a pinch of salt.

7 Drain the potatoes, return them to their pot, and add the butter and a pinch of salt, swirling until the potatoes are coated.

8 To make the herby tahini sauce, blend all the ingredients in a food processor or blender until very smooth.

9 Divide the farro between four wide, shallow bowls, and arrange the vegetables, potatoes, and eggs on top. Drizzle generously with the herby tahini sauce. Serve with pickled onions and hot sauce.

COZY KITCHARI

WITH CILANTRO-TAHINI SAUCE

Gentle, cozy, and warm with aromatics like turmeric and fresh ginger, kitchari is an easy-to-digest ancient Ayurvedic staple, often an Indian baby's first taste of solid food and a mother's remedy for her sick family. The rice and *moong dal* (a split mung bean that looks like a yellow lentil) cook down into a creamy porridge that was most likely the inspiration behind the Spice Girls' smash hit "2 Become 1." There are infinite ways to make kitchari, with sizzled Indian spices like cumin and mustard seeds or topped with yogurt. My version is finished with a big squeeze of lemon, a drizzle of cilantro-tahini sauce, and a jumble of vegetables. I like a mix of roasted, sautéed, and steamed vegetables, such as carrots, cauliflower, broccoli, broccolini, winter squash, greens, zucchini, leeks, or peas.

Makes 4 bowls

FOR THE KITCHARI:

1 tablespoon coconut oil

1 (2-inch) knob of ginger, peeled and grated or finely minced

1 large garlic clove, grated or finely minced

1 teaspoon turmeric powder

½ cup moong dal (see Note)

½ cup basmati or jasmine rice, rinsed until water runs clear

5 cups water, plus more as needed

1 teaspoon salt, plus more to taste

1 tablespoon freshly squeezed lemon juice, plus more to taste

FOR THE VEGETABLE TOPPING:

2 to 3 pounds mixed vegetables of your choosing

Coconut oil or olive oil for sautéing and roasting, plus more as needed

Salt, for seasoning

Lemon wedges, for serving

FOR THE CILANTRO-TAHINI SAUCE:

¼ cup roughly chopped fresh cilantro with stems

¼ cup tahini, plus more to taste

2 tablespoons to ¼ cup cold water

2 tablespoons freshly squeezed lemon juice

1 large garlic clove

½ a medium jalapeño, seeded

½ teaspoon salt

NOTE: Split yellow mung beans (moong dal) are available at Indian or Asian markets, some health food stores, or online.

CONTINUED

1 Preheat the oven to 425 degrees F (if roasting your vegetables).

2 Melt the coconut oil over medium heat in a large pot or Dutch oven. Add the ginger, garlic, and turmeric and sauté gently until soft, stirring constantly and turning down the heat if it starts to brown. Add the moong dal, rice, and water to the pot, scraping all the bits off the bottom of the pot with a wooden spoon.

3 Bring to a boil, then immediately lower the heat to a gentle, bubbling simmer (low or medium low). Cook uncovered, stirring every few minutes to prevent sticking, until the rice and dal melt into a soft, creamy porridge, around 40 minutes. Add more water as needed. The rice and dal should be indistinguishable from one another. Season with salt and lemon juice.

4 To make the vegetable topping, while the kitchari cooks, roast and sauté your vegetables in the coconut oil and season with salt. Roast for 30 to 40 minutes, flipping halfway through, until they're tender and have some nice browning and crisp edges.

5 Meanwhile, make the sauce. Combine the cilantro, tahini, 2 tablespoons of cold water, lemon juice, garlic, jalapeño, and salt in a small food processor or blender until smooth and creamy. If you'd like a thinner sauce, add more cold water a teaspoon at a time. Taste and add more tahini if it's not strong enough.

6 When the kitchari and roasted vegetables are about 10 minutes away from being done, lightly sauté any greens with a little coconut oil or olive oil and salt. If not roasting or sautéing your vegetables, steam them until crisp-tender.

7 Plop the kitchari into bowls and top with the vegetables and drizzles of the cilantro-tahini sauce. Serve with lemon wedges and more sauce on the side.

VIETNAMESE FRESH ROLLS
WITH TAHINI-HOISIN DIPPING SAUCE

Fresh rolls might be the easiest Vietnamese or Thai restaurant dish to perfectly replicate at home. But rolling these in advance can lead to frustration: the rice paper often sticks to the plate and tears when lifted, causing the filling to burst from the wrapper. My solution is not only less work for you, it's a fun, interactive experience for your tablemates: place a wide bowl of warm water in the center of the table (I use a 9.5-inch glass pie pan), put out a plate or two of prepared fillings, and teach your guests how to roll their own "to order." If you *insist* on making them in advance, store each roll separately so they don't stick together, and don't refrigerate for longer than an hour, to prevent drying and cracking. Fresh rolls are super versatile; swap out the shrimp for strips of fried tofu (precooked from the Asian market), chunks of salmon, extra veggies like steamed asparagus or strips of daikon radish, or slices of leftover Gingery Chicken Meatballs with Sesame Chili Crisp Glaze (page 101).

Makes 8 fresh rolls

FOR THE ROLLS:

7 to 8 ounces thin rice noodles
(half a standard package)
8 round rice paper wrappers, plus
more in case of tearing
1 dozen large cooked shrimp,
shells and tails removed, sliced
in half horizontally

1 large bunch fresh mixed tender
herbs, such as Thai basil, mint,
or shiso, stems removed
1 small English cucumber, sliced into
long, thin strips with a mandoline
or vegetable peeler
1 large carrot, peeled and shaved
into long strips with a mandoline
or vegetable peeler

FOR THE TAHINI-HOISIN DIPPING SAUCE:

¼ cup freshly squeezed lime juice (from 2 to 3 limes)

¼ cup plus 2 tablespoons tahini

3 tablespoons hoisin sauce

3½ teaspoons soy sauce

1 tablespoon unseasoned rice vinegar

1 to 4 tablespoons cold water

Sriracha (optional)

1 Cook the rice noodles according to package directions, drain, and rinse well with cold water.

2 Meanwhile, make the dipping sauce: in a small bowl, mix the lime juice, tahini, hoisin, soy sauce, rice vinegar, and 1 tablespoon of cold water (adding more water as needed) until it's a smooth, dippable consistency. Squeeze in a little sriracha if you like spice. Set aside.

3 Fill a large, wide bowl with warm water. Working one at a time, submerge a sheet of rice paper for about 5 seconds. It will still be a bit firm but will soften up as the water absorbs. Lay it on a flat surface, carefully unfolding any edges that may have curled.

4 To build a roll, line up 3 shrimp halves on the widest part of the lower third of the rice paper and layer the herbs, a plank of cucumber, a couple carrot strips, and a small bundle of noodles on top, leaving at least an inch on both sides. Overstuffing will lead to tearing, so be conservative until you get a feel for it.

5 Fold the tab of rice paper closest to you tightly over the stuffing and roll once, using your fingers to pull the stuffing in tight. Fold the left and right sides in like you're making a burrito and continue rolling tightly but gently, careful not to rip the rice paper.

6 Serve with the dipping sauce and enjoy immediately.

COLD SESAME SOBA

WITH SUMMER VEG

Keep your pasta salad! I'll take the slippery slurp of a cold Asian noodle dish any day. My version of this classic Japanese soba preparation heroically attempts to dwindle down your zucchini stash, assuming your garden's summer squash is just as infamously prolific as mine. But this salad also sings without the vegetables, with just a simple garnish of sesame seeds and green onions if you're looking for a quick, simple, flavorful lunch. She also plays well at potlucks and picnics; the noodles only get tastier as they sit and mingle with the dressing.

Makes 4 servings as a main dish and 6 to 8 as a side

1 small bunch (6 to 8 leaves) kale, ribs and stems removed

4 bundles (around 400 g) soba noodles

Salt, for sprinkling

3 tablespoons plus 1 teaspoon sesame oil, divided

3 tablespoons soy sauce

1 tablespoon honey

1 tablespoon sesame seeds

1 teaspoon sriracha (optional)

Neutral oil, for sautéing

2 medium zucchini, sliced into ¼-inch coins

2 green onions, white and green parts thinly sliced on the bias

CONTINUED →

1   Bring a large pot of salted water to a boil. Add the kale and blanch for a minute or two, until bright green and softened. Reserving the kale water, transfer the kale to a strainer using tongs and run it under cold water to stop the cooking.

2   Cook the soba noodles in the kale water according to package directions, until al dente.

3   While the noodles are cooking, squeeze out as much water as possible from the kale and slice the kale blob into ½-inch ribbons. Sprinkle lightly with salt, drizzle with 1 teaspoon of the sesame oil, and lightly massage it into the kale. Set aside.

4   Drain the soba noodles and rinse with cold water until the noodles are cold. Set aside.

5   In a large serving bowl, add 3 tablespoons of sesame oil, the soy sauce, honey, sesame seeds, and sriracha and whisk until the honey has completely dissolved. Add the soba noodles, tossing until the noodles are evenly coated.

6   Add 2 teaspoons of the neutral oil to a large pan heated to medium high, and sauté the zucchini in a single layer until both sides are deeply browned, seasoning with a light sprinkle of salt on each side. This will most likely need to be done in batches. Add 2 more teaspoons of oil before starting each batch. Transfer the zucchini to a plate to cool.

7   Add the green onions, kale, and zucchini to the soba noodles, tossing carefully to keep the zucchini intact. If you have the time, let the noodles marinate for a few hours. If you can't, it can be eaten immediately. Leftovers are tasty both cold and at room temperature.

BEEF ARAYES

WITH GARLICKY TAHINI SAUCE

Like many contentious Middle Eastern dishes, arayes have been claimed by many countries and cultures as their invention. Depending on who you ask, they're from Turkey, Lebanon, Jordan, Palestine, or Syria, and they have become a popular street food in Israel. This sandwich is unusual in that you stuff the pita with raw meat *before* you cook it, until it's juicy on the inside and crisp on the outside. Make sure you pick up pita bread with deep pockets, rather than thicker flat breads deceptively labeled as "Greek pita." The bright, zingy tahini sauce is the perfect counter to the rich, warmly spiced meat.

Makes 2 to 4 servings

1 pound ground beef (not lean)

¼ small yellow onion, finely minced

1 large or 2 small garlic cloves,
    finely minced

⅓ cup chopped fresh parsley

1½ teaspoons smoked paprika

1 teaspoon ground coriander

1 teaspoon ground allspice

1 teaspoon ground cumin

1 teaspoon ground cinnamon

1 teaspoon salt

2 (7 to 8 inches across) pita pockets,
    sliced in half

1 batch Garlicky Tahini Sauce
    (page 63)

CONTINUED →

1 Preheat the oven to 400 degrees F.

2 In a large bowl, mix the ground beef, onion, garlic, parsley, spices, and salt with your hands until evenly incorporated. Fill each pita half with one-quarter of the meat mixture, making sure they're evenly filled from the bottom to the top edge.

3 Place a baking sheet on the bottom rack of the oven and bake the pitas directly on the middle rack above. This will catch any drippings but allow the pita to get crispy on both sides. Bake for about 10 minutes, until the meat is cooked through and the pita is crisp.

4 While the arayes bake, make the Garlicky Tahini Sauce.

5 Cut the arayes in half and serve immediately with the tahini sauce for dipping or drizzling.

CHALLAH CHICKEN SCHNITZEL

"SHABBAT SANDWICHES"

I was washing dishes and listening to my favorite Jewish podcast, *Unorthodox*, when I was stopped in my tracks by a sandwich. A trendy Israeli sandwich created only a few years ago in Tel Aviv that, rudely, no one had bothered to tell me about! The show's cohost mentioned it in passing—"challah with schnitzel"—and that was enough to send me straight to the grocery store. The "Shabbat Sandwich," named after the Friday night Sabbath when Jews typically eat challah, is thick slices of squishy challah sandwiching crispy chicken schnitzel, fried eggplant, tahini, Israeli pickle, and a mighty shmear of matbucha, a Moroccan tomato pepper relish. Preparing this sandwich is a bit of a project, but you can make a lot of the components a day or two in advance. Be aware that some bakeries only sell challah on Fridays. Instead of slicing the bread, you can also serve it as one giant challah choagie cut up party style!

Makes 4 sandwiches

Neutral oil, for frying

1 large Japanese or Chinese eggplant, cut into 16 to 24 (¼-inch) slices

1 teaspoon salt, divided, plus more to taste

¼ to ½ cup all-purpose flour

2 large eggs

½ cup panko bread crumbs

6 tablespoons untoasted sesame seeds

2 chicken breasts (1.5 pounds total)

1 loaf fresh challah, sliced into 8 (1-inch) slices from the widest part of the loaf (bonus points for sesame-crusted challah!)

½ cup matbucha (page 91)

4 Israeli pickles, sliced lengthwise into thirds (optional; see Note)

1 batch Garlicky Tahini Sauce (page 63)

NOTE: Israeli pickles are typically sold in cans in Middle Eastern markets or online. They are full-sour, far more puckery than a dill pickle, chartreuse, and on the softer side of crisp.

CONTINUED →

1   Heat ¼ inch of neutral oil in a large pan over medium high. Fry the eggplant in a single layer until browned on both sides, 10 to 12 minutes total, and transfer to a cooling rack or a plate lined with a paper towel. Season with salt to taste. You may need to fry in batches. Turn off the heat and reserve the oil in the pan; you'll use it for the chicken.

2   Set up your workstation with three plates or shallow bowls. Mix ¼ cup of the flour and ¼ teaspoon of the salt in one plate, adding more flour later as needed. Beat 2 eggs with ¼ teaspoon salt in the second plate, and mix the panko, sesame seeds, and ¼ teaspoon salt in the last plate.

3   Place a chicken breast inside a large ziplock bag or between two sheets of plastic wrap, and pound with a mallet or rolling pin until it's ½ inch thick. Repeat with the second chicken breast. They will be very large!

4   Press both sides of the chicken into the flour mixture on the first plate, shaking off any excess, then dip both sides into the egg plate, letting the excess drip off. Finally, press it into the panko and sesame seeds plate, making sure it's completely coated and sticking.

5   Add more oil to the pan so it's back at the ¼-inch mark, and heat to medium high. When the oil is hot, add one chicken breast to the pan. Cook for 3 to 5 minutes on each side, until very golden brown and crispy, and transfer to a cooling rack. Sprinkle with salt to taste. Repeat with the second chicken breast, adding more oil and letting it heat up in between batches if needed.

6   Cut each chicken breast in half. Spread each of the four bottom bread slices with about 2 tablespoons of the matbucha. Top each slice with half of a chicken breast, 4 to 6 eggplant slices, several Israeli pickle slices, and a healthy drizzle of tahini sauce. Top with the other slices of bread and eat immediately!

Matbucha

Matbucha is a slightly spicy Moroccan tomato-pepper relish often found snuggled up next to other cold salads, spreads, and olives on Middle Eastern and North African tables, just waiting to be swiped up with fresh bread or pita. If matbucha sounds new to you, it might be more familiar than you think: it's also the base for *shakshuka*! Leftovers can be warmed in a pan and thinned out with a little tomato puree or water before you crack a few eggs in to steam. The matbucha can be prepared a day or two before the Shabbat sandwiches, stored in a sealed container in the fridge.

Makes ¾ cup

½ red bell pepper

½ green bell pepper

1 small Anaheim chile

1 very small or ½ medium jalapeño, seeded

2 tablespoons olive oil

2 medium garlic cloves, minced

1½ teaspoons smoked paprika

1 cup (8 ounces; about half a small can) crushed tomatoes

¼ teaspoon salt

1   Char the red and green bell peppers, Anaheim chile, and jalapeño until their skins are completely black, either directly over a flame on a gas stove, on the direct flames of a grill, or on the top rack of your oven under the broiler.

2   Transfer them to a paper bag (grocery bag works great) and roll down the top so they can steam inside for 15 minutes. Once cool enough to handle, peel the skin off the peppers and remove any remaining stems and seeds. Finely chop the peppers.

CONTINUED →

3   In a small saucepan over medium heat, heat the oil. Add the garlic and paprika
    and sauté for about a minute, stirring frequently, until the garlic is fragrant but
    not crispy. Stir in the tomatoes, charred peppers, and salt, and lower the heat
    to medium low. Let it simmer partially covered for 30 to 45 minutes, stirring
    every 5 to 10 minutes to make sure nothing sticks. It's ready when it's thick
    and jammy.

4   Cover and set aside until room temp or cool. Keep tightly lidded in the fridge for
    up to 3 days.

    NOTE: Double the batch if you want enough leftovers to make shakshuka.

BASIL-LIME PASTA

WITH
SESAME CHICKEN BOLOGNESE

Cashews are magic. Blitzed with fistfuls of basil and enough lime to stave off a sailor's scurvy, they create a creamy, velvety sauce that clings to pasta with so many curves, grooves, and nooks that they belong on the cover of a pretentious architecture magazine. Combined with umami-packed ground chicken, it eats like a tangy Asian Bolognese. This pasta, inspired by a sauce from recipe developer Anna Stockwell, is a favorite dinner party meal, rounded out with crisp-tender green beans, and everybody always goes back for seconds.

Makes 4 to 6 servings

1¼ cups roasted, salted cashews, divided

1¼ cups boiling water

1 pound short pasta with lots of folds and ridges, like cascatelli, radiatore, fusilli, or rigatoni

2 tablespoons sesame oil, divided

4 medium garlic cloves, minced

1 pound ground chicken (not lean, if possible)

1 tablespoon tahini

1 tablespoon fish sauce

1 tablespoon soy sauce

2 teaspoons sriracha

A pinch of sugar

2 teaspoons unseasoned rice vinegar

2 cups fresh basil leaves

Zest of 1 small lime

⅓ cup freshly squeezed lime juice, plus more to taste (from 1 to 3 limes)

1 large jalapeño, seeded

2 teaspoons salt, divided, plus more to taste

¾ pound fresh green beans, trimmed and cut into bite-size pieces

Lime wedges, for serving

 CONTINUED →

1 Add 1 cup of the cashews and the boiling water to your blender pitcher and let soak for 20 to 30 minutes.

2 While the cashews soak, start cooking at step 3. About 15 minutes into the soaking time, put a large pot of salted water on high heat and cook the pasta a minute less than package directions, or until the pasta is al dente.

3 Meanwhile, heat 1 tablespoon of the sesame oil in a large skillet over medium heat and add the garlic, stirring constantly for 30 seconds until fragrant, being careful not to brown or burn. Add the ground chicken and break into smaller chunks using a wooden spoon. When the chicken is no longer pink, add the tahini, fish sauce, soy sauce, sriracha, and sugar, and stir to combine. Sauté for a minute or two until the chicken is cooked through. Turn off the heat and stir in the vinegar, scraping the bottom of the pan to release any sticky bits. Transfer the chicken to a bowl and cover to keep warm.

4 Return to your blender and add the basil, lime zest, lime juice, jalapeño, and 1½ teaspoons of the salt to the soaked cashews (do not drain the water) and blend until completely smooth, creamy, and bright green with no specks of basil remaining. If you don't have a high-powered blender, this could take several minutes.

5 In the same pan that you cooked the chicken, heat the remaining 1 tablespoon sesame oil over medium heat and add the green beans. Sprinkle with the remaining ½ teaspoon salt and stir-fry for a few minutes, until bright green and crisp-tender.

6 Drain the pasta, reserving 1 cup of pasta water. Return the pasta to its pot, stir in the lime-basil sauce and ¼ cup pasta water, adding more water if the sauce is too thick or needs to be creamier. Heat the pot over low and stir in the ground chicken until everything is warm. Taste and season with more salt, lime juice, or pasta water as needed. Stir in the green beans. Chop the remaining ¼ cup of cashews and sprinkle on top of the pasta. Serve with lime wedges.

STEAK TACOS

WITH

CHARRED CORN—SESAME RELISH

This zippy little corn relish was adapted from a recipe by South Carolina chef Shuai Wang, printed in *Bon Appétit* magazine, and it's truly the star of this taco show. Bright, acidic, and bold, when freshly shucked corn is in season it's just as delicious as a salad topped with slices of steak and cubes of avocado. Which is why this recipe makes a bit more than you need for tacos; I predict you'll be very happy to have leftovers. (Why yes, I *am* a corn relish psychic.) Fresh corn is best, but frozen will get you through the winter. Keeping with the summer theme, the corn and steak can also be cooked on a grill; just char the corn on the cob and then cut it off. If steak's not your thing, this is equally delicious with shrimp or salmon.

 CONTINUED →

Makes 4 to 6 tacos

1 pound strip steak (sometimes called top loin strip or top sirloin) or hanger steak, at least 1 inch thick

1 teaspoon salt, divided, plus more to taste

3 to 4 teaspoons toasted sesame oil, divided

2 large ears of corn, husked (or 1¾ cups frozen, defrosted corn)

2 to 3 limes

1½ tablespoons olive oil

1½ teaspoons soy sauce

1 teaspoon chili crisp (preferably Lao Gan Ma)

1 teaspoon unseasoned rice vinegar

1 small shallot, thinly sliced

1 small jalapeño, very finely diced (about 2 tablespoons)

¼ cup chopped fresh cilantro

1 tablespoon toasted sesame seeds

1 large garlic clove, grated or finely minced

½ teaspoon high smoke-point oil, such as avocado, canola, or safflower

1 avocado

4 to 6 corn tortillas or small soft taco-size flour tortillas (Caramelo makes the absolute best flour tortillas and can be ordered from their website)

¼ cup crumbled queso fresca or cotija cheese

Hot sauce, for serving (optional)

1 Season the steak on both sides with ½ teaspoon salt and 1 teaspoon of the sesame oil, rubbing it in with your fingers. Set aside to marinate. If you can salt the steak hours in advance, it will have even more flavor.

2 Cut the kernels off the cobs of corn (see Tip). Heat a cast-iron skillet over medium high and add the kernels, pressing them down with a spatula so they lightly char. After 3 to 5 minutes, stir the corn and char the other sides. If you're not using cast iron, add a teaspoon of sesame oil to the pan before adding the corn. Transfer the corn to a plate to cool and wipe out the pan to use later.

3 Squeeze 1 to 2 limes until you have a scant ¼ cup juice, and quarter the remaining lime to serve later. In a medium bowl, mix the lime juice, olive oil, the remaining 2 teaspoons sesame oil, soy sauce, chili crisp, rice vinegar, and a pinch of salt. Mix in the shallots, jalapeño, cilantro, sesame seeds, and garlic. Add the corn and mix well. Taste and season with a touch more salt as needed. Pop the corn relish into the fridge to marinate.

4 Heat the pan over high until smoking hot, about 5 minutes. Add the high smoke-point oil and carefully lower in the steak. Cook until medium rare, 3 to 4 minutes on each side, until the internal temperature reads 130 degrees F. Remove the steak and let it rest for 10 minutes.

5 Meanwhile, make the guacamole. In a small bowl, smash the avocado with a fork, squeeze in juice from a quarter of a lime, and add a pinch of salt. Taste and continue adding salt and lime until it tastes perfect to you.

6 Warm the tortillas in a pan, or directly on a flame, until pliable, and wrap in a dish towel to keep warm.

7 Cut the steak into ½-inch slices, then cut the strips into bite-size pieces.

8 To assemble the tacos, spread some guacamole onto each tortilla and add the equivalent of two slices of steak, a scoop of corn relish, and a sprinkle of cheese. Serve with lime wedges and your favorite hot sauce.

TIP: I use a Bundt pan to keep the kernels from flying everywhere! Insert the pointed tip of the corn into the hole in the middle of the Bundt pan and run your knife down the cob to release the kernels.

GINGERY CHICKEN MEATBALLS

WITH

SESAME CHILI CRISP GLAZE

Spin a pound of ground meat and seasonings into a meatloaf and you have . . . dinner. Form those exact same ingredients into meatballs and watch as they're enthusiastically gobbled up. Ground chicken has become my all-around preferred mince; it cooks up juicier and more tender than turkey, and its mild profile allows the greatest hits of Asian flavors to shine through in these bold and flavorful meatballs. Serve with steamed rice and a simply stir-fried vegetable, like bok choy or asparagus, or as a party snack accessorized with frilly toothpicks for a vintage vibe.

Makes around 22 meatballs and 3 to 4 servings as a main dish

FOR THE MEATBALLS:

1 egg

3 tablespoons minced fresh
   cilantro, divided

1 tablespoon soy sauce

1 tablespoon chili crisp (preferably
   Lao Gan Ma)

½ teaspoon salt

¼ teaspoon white pepper

2 tablespoons sesame oil, divided

1 (2-inch) chunk of ginger, peeled and
   grated or finely minced

2 large garlic cloves, grated or
   finely minced

2 green onions, white and green parts
   thinly sliced, divided

1 pound ground chicken (not lean)

¼ cup panko bread crumbs

1 tablespoon neutral oil

1 tablespoon toasted sesame seeds

FOR THE GLAZE:

3 tablespoons tahini

3 tablespoons mirin

2 tablespoons soy sauce

2 tablespoons honey

1 tablespoon chili crisp (preferably
   Lao Gan Ma)

1 tablespoon water

1½ teaspoons unseasoned rice vinegar

1 teaspoon toasted sesame oil

 CONTINUED →

1   To make the meatballs, in a medium bowl, mix 1 tablespoon of the sesame oil, ginger, garlic, 1 green onion, egg, 2 tablespoons cilantro, soy sauce, chili crisp, salt, and white pepper. Add in the ground chicken and the panko and mix until thoroughly incorporated. Chill in the refrigerator for 20 to 30 minutes.

2   Using wet hands, form the meat mixture into 1½-inch balls. They will be quite loose and sticky; don't worry, they'll firm up while cooking! Heat a large pan over medium high and add the remaining tablespoon of sesame oil and the neutral oil. Once the oil has spread, add the meatballs to the pan; you may need to cook in batches. Turn the heat down to medium and brown the meatballs on all sides, 2 to 3 minutes. Turn the heat down to low and cover until cooked through, 2 to 3 more minutes. Transfer the meatballs to a serving bowl.

3   To make the glaze, add all of the glaze ingredients to a small saucepan. Gently heat over medium low until it's thick enough to coat the back of a spoon, about 5 minutes. Pour the glaze over the meatballs and toss to coat. Garnish with the sesame seeds, the remaining scallion, and the remaining tablespoon of cilantro.

WEEKNIGHT POKE BOWLS

There are certain dishes I think of as Restaurant Food. Meals that seem too complicated to cook at home, composed of expensive, hard-to-find ingredients, that use intimidating techniques. I had put poke in this category. So when a friend who only cooks simple dishes with minimal ingredients served me a wildly delicious, vibrant bowl of poke in his very own home, I was gobsmacked by how incredibly easy and affordable it could be. When I want a beautiful bowl of food to impress guests, this is what I serve. I've also brought this poke on an airplane and made it in a camper-van! If you have a bottle of high-quality soy sauce in the pantry, this is its big moment. Dress the fish just before serving; marinating can make the fish mushy.

Makes 2 bowls

1 cup short-grain Japanese white rice

½ pound sushi-grade tuna, salmon, or a mix of both, or pre-cubed frozen, defrosted tuna or salmon (see Note)

1 avocado

2 teaspoons soy sauce

2 teaspoons sesame oil

½ teaspoon sriracha (optional)

2 tablespoons finely minced yellow or sweet onion (from ½ small onion)

2 tablespoons jalapeño, finely diced, seeded (from 1 medium-large jalapeño)

2 teaspoons toasted sesame seeds, divided (white, black, or a mix)

Salt (bonus if you have Hawaiian sea salt!)

½ cup prepared Japanese seaweed salad (also called wakame)

½ cup shelled edamame

Pickled ginger, for serving (optional)

NOTE: You can find sushi-grade salmon and tuna at Asian markets, and you can find affordable, pre-cubed frozen fish at some grocery stores or online at FreshSeas.com.

 CONTINUED→

1   Cook the rice per package directions. Fluff the rice and let it cool slightly so it's warm or room temperature when served.

2   While the rice cooks, remove the skin from the fish and cut it into ¾-inch to 1-inch cubes. Set aside in a mixing bowl.

3   Cut the avocado into cubes or, if you want a fancy Instagram-worthy avocado fan, cut the avocado in half, remove the pit, and carefully peel off the skin. Place the halves flat side down and cut into thin slices, lengthwise, holding the avocado together. Use all your fingers to lightly push on the wide end of the avocado so it fans out. Leave the fans on the cutting board.

4   Mix the fish with the soy sauce, sesame oil, and sriracha, then mix in the onion, jalapeño, and 1 teaspoon of the sesame seeds. Taste and lightly season with salt as needed.

5   Scoop a bed of rice into two wide, shallow bowls. Top each with a mound of poke, ¼ cup seaweed salad, ¼ cup edamame, and some pickled ginger. Slide a chef's knife underneath the avocado fan and gently transfer it to the rice. Sprinkle with salt. Sprinkle the remaining teaspoon of sesame seeds over the avocado and rice. Serve immediately with chopsticks.

CRISPY SESAME SCHNITZEL'D OYSTER MUSHROOMS

Mushrooms are my biggest farmers' market splurge. Every Sunday I try to hurry past the Sno-Valley Mushrooms stand at my neighborhood farmers' market, but the eye-catching clusters of shiitakes and cinnamon caps, with their cute little toadstool faces, call out to me, "Hiiiii, Rachel! We're *only* eight dollllaaaars!" I'm a sucker for the big bouquets of velvety blue oyster mushrooms that cook up super tender and meaty. Here they are given the schnitzel treatment: breaded and quickly fried until crunchy, never greasy, super juicy, and extremely delicious. Serve with lemon wedges and a little arugula salad—simply dressed with olive oil, lemon, and salt—and mashed potatoes for a heartier meal.

Makes 4 generous portions

1 pound fresh oyster mushrooms (not king oysters), dirt brushed off with a dry dish towel
½ cup all-purpose flour
Kosher salt
2 to 3 large eggs
½ to ¾ cup panko bread crumbs

½ to ¾ cup untoasted sesame seeds
8 thyme sprigs, leaves stripped and chopped, stems discarded
Neutral oil, for frying
Flaky salt, for sprinkling
1 large lemon, cut into quarters

1 Trim any dry bits off the foot of the mushrooms and pull the clusters apart until they're completely separated. Cut any particularly large mushrooms in half lengthwise.

2 Line up three plates or shallow bowls for the dredging process. Mix the flour and a generous pinch of kosher salt in the plate on the left. Crack 2 of the eggs into the middle plate, add a pinch of salt, and use a fork to whisk the eggs. Mix ½ cup of the panko, sesame seeds, thyme, and a pinch of salt in the plate on the right.

3 Press both sides of a mushroom into the flour and shake off the excess. Drag it through the egg, making sure all sides are covered, and let the excess drip off. Press it into the panko mixture, making sure all parts of the mushroom are completely coated. Place on a plate or baking sheet and repeat with the rest of the mushrooms, adding more egg, panko, and sesame seeds to the plates as needed.

4 Heat ½ inch of oil in a large pan over medium high. When a tiny flick of water into the oil sizzles, add the mushrooms to the pan. Don't crowd the pan; this will most likely need to be done in batches. Cook on both sides until deeply golden, 1 to 2 minutes per side. If they get dark too fast, turn down the heat.

5 Transfer the mushrooms to a paper towel–lined plate or a cooling rack, and sprinkle with flaky salt. Serve immediately with generous squeezes of lemon!

CHOCOLATE MISO
WHOOPIE PIES
WITH TAHINI CREAM

A fact I think about often: Whoopi Goldberg named herself after the whoopee cushion when she was repeatedly teased for passing gas on stage. A comforting fact: There are zero farts in these whoopie pies! A third fact? Whoopie pies aren't pies at all. They are tender little cakes usually sandwiching buttercream or marshmallow fluff. These whoopie pies are filled with fluffy whipped cream, sweetened with maple, and flavored with nutty tahini. Turns out, miso, chocolate, and tahini are a match made in dessert heaven; if you don't love a saccharine dessert, you'll appreciate the balance of salty miso and lightly sweetened cream.

Makes 5 sandwiches

1 cup all-purpose flour

¼ cup unsweetened Dutch-process
   cocoa powder, sifted

1 teaspoon baking soda

¼ cup unsalted butter, softened

¼ cup granulated sugar

¼ cup loosely packed
   brown sugar

1 large egg

2 tablespoons yellow miso paste

1 teaspoon vanilla extract

¼ cup whole milk

¼ cup plain Greek yogurt

1 batch Tahini Whipped Cream
   (page 113)

CONTINUED →

1 Preheat the oven to 350 degrees F. Line two 13-by-18-inch baking sheets with parchment paper, and spray with nonstick cooking spray.

2 In a small bowl, mix the flour, cocoa, and baking soda and set aside. In a stand mixer or in a large bowl with an electric hand mixer, cream the butter and sugars until fluffy, about 2 to 3 minutes. Scrape down the sides of the bowl with a spatula.

3 Add the egg, miso, and vanilla, and mix on medium until incorporated. Add the milk and Greek yogurt and mix on low until just incorporated. Add dry ingredients to the wet ingredients and mix on medium until just combined.

4 Make ten cakes by plopping 3 tablespoons of batter in tall, rounded heaps onto the prepared baking sheets, 2 inches apart. The little cakes will spread as they bake! Bake for 10 minutes, on the center rack, until a toothpick comes out clean. Remove from the oven and lift the corners of the parchment paper to transfer to a cooling rack. Let cool completely.

5 While the cakes cool, make the tahini whipped cream.

6 Lay out five cakes, flat side up, and spread each with 3 tablespoons of whipped cream (or more, if you wish) all the way to the edges. Top each with a cake lid and eat immediately. Leftover cake can be stored in a sealed container on the counter for 2 days and filled with freshly whipped cream just before eating.

Tahini Whipped Cream

I like to squirt canned whipped cream directly into my mouth as much as the next person, but there's nothing like a cloud of freshly whipped cream plopped over a bowl of fresh berries. Sweetened with maple and lightly flavored with tahini, here's a nutty, slightly more complex twist on the classic.

Makes about 2 cups

1 cup heavy cream

2 tablespoons real maple syrup

3 tablespoons tahini

1 Using a hand mixer, stand mixer, or a good old–fashioned whisk and elbow grease, beat the cream with the maple syrup until medium–to–stiff peaks form. Gently fold in the tahini with a spatula until fully incorporated.

2 Keep refrigerated in a tightly lidded container until ready to use. Use the whipped cream the same day it's made.

TAHINI FRANGIPANE APRICOT GALETTE

Excuse me! Are you roasting your apricots? If not, consider this a public service announcement. Instead of tossing your underripe, flavorless, slightly mealy, a-little-bit-mushy apricots into the compost, toss them into a hot oven and prepare to swoon. Better yet, toss them onto a galette with a creamy, nutty layer of tahini frangipane! Don't let all these fancy French words scare you; this dessert is rustic, light, and easy to assemble, especially if you use a good-quality store-bought pie crust. If you can't find apricots, sub in plums, pluots, or peaches.

Makes one 10-inch galette

FOR THE FRANGIPANE:

¼ cup tahini

2 tablespoons salted butter, softened and cut into smaller chunks

2 tablespoons sugar

1 egg, beaten well and divided

1 teaspoon vanilla extract or paste

1 teaspoon lemon zest

¼ teaspoon ground nutmeg

FOR THE GALETTE:

1 pound apricots

1 prepared pie dough round, store-bought or homemade (I like Trader Joe's all-butter crust)

2 tablespoons flour

1 to 2 tablespoons plus 1 teaspoon sugar, divided

½ teaspoon ground cinnamon

1 teaspoon untoasted sesame seeds

Flaky salt, for sprinkling

1 Line a baking sheet with parchment paper.

2 To make the frangipane, using a hand mixer in a small bowl, beat the tahini, butter, and sugar at medium high speed until completely combined, smooth, creamy. Add half of the beaten egg, the vanilla, lemon zest, and nutmeg, and continue to beat until well combined and smooth. Chill in the fridge for 30 minutes.

3 Meanwhile, slice the apricots into half-inch rounds, removing the pit when you get to it. Transfer to a bowl and set aside.

4 Place a rack in the lower third of the oven and preheat to 425 degrees F.

5 Roll the pie dough into approximately a 12-inch-wide, ⅛- to ¼-inch-thick round and transfer it to the lined baking sheet.

6 When the frangipane is ready, spread it onto the pie dough (an offset spatula works great here), leaving a 2-inch border around the edge.

7 Add the flour, 1 tablespoon sugar, and cinnamon to the bowl with the apricots and toss to coat. I prefer a lightly sweetened dessert, but if you'd like something sweeter, double up on the sugar.

8 Arrange the apricots on top of the frangipane, maintaining the border. Fold the edges of the dough over the fruit, letting it naturally overlap, and transfer the galette to the fridge to firm up, about 20 minutes.

9 Brush the remainder of the beaten egg onto the crust (you won't need all of it), and sprinkle with the remaining 1 teaspoon sugar, the sesame seeds, and a little flaky salt. Gently press the sesame seeds into the dough.

10 Bake on the bottom rack until deeply brown, crisp on the bottom, and bubbling, 40 to 50 minutes. Transfer to a cooling rack and enjoy warm or at room temp. Leftovers will keep covered in the fridge for 5 days.

TENDER TAHINI ALMOND CAKE

WITH STRAWBERRIES AND CREAM

There are two kinds of cake people in this world: the light-and-fluffies and those who like to sink their fork into a dense, moist crumb. I am firmly in the second category. This simple one-bowl cake adapted (read: tahinified) from Sweet Laurel, a grain-free, dairy-free, refined-sugar-free bakery in Los Angeles, bakes up impossibly tender thanks to almond flour. Try to bake a dry cake with almond flour! I dare you! Strawberries are a lovely topping, but imagine if you found yourself with a couple perfectly ripe summer peaches or a carton of farmers' market raspberries! You know what to do.

Makes one 8-inch round or loaf cake

2 tablespoons solid coconut oil, plus more for greasing the pan

2 large eggs

½ cup real maple syrup

2 tablespoons tahini

1 teaspoon vanilla extract

Zest of 1 small lemon (about a tablespoon plus a teaspoon)

2½ cups almond flour

½ teaspoon baking soda

½ teaspoon salt

1 batch Tahini Whipped Cream (page 113)

½ pound fresh strawberries, hulled and sliced or medium diced

CONTINUED →

1   Preheat the oven to 350 degrees F.

2   Line the bottom of an 8-inch round pan, or the bottom and sides of a loaf pan, with parchment paper and grease any sides the paper doesn't touch with coconut oil or baking spray.

3   In a medium bowl, whisk the eggs until fluffy. Add the maple syrup, tahini, coconut oil, vanilla, and lemon zest, and whisk, mashing the coconut oil into smaller bits but not worrying about the lumps that remain. Mix in the almond flour, baking soda, and salt until just incorporated. The batter will be thick.

4   Scrape the batter into the prepared cake pan, and smooth the top with a rubber spatula. If using a round pan, bake for 30 minutes. Bake for 40 to 45 minutes in a loaf pan, until a toothpick comes out clean. Cool the cake completely before removing it from the pan.

5   While the cake bakes, prepare the tahini whipped cream and store it covered in the fridge until ready to serve.

6   Spread the whipped cream on top of the cake and cover it with the sliced strawberries. Leftover cake is good in the fridge for 1 day, longer if it's not covered in cream.

NO-BAKE
BERRY TAHINI
LAYER BARS

I have to get something off my chest. *takes deep breath* This is a raw, vegan dessert. Wait! Please don't turn the page! While "raw" and "vegan" are obviously draws for some, others assume they'll be settling for a sad, unsatisfying facsimile of their favorite treat. I fell in love with raw, vegan desserts when I traveled to New Zealand, where nearly every café I visited, no matter how tiny the town, had a cold case full of beautiful, surprisingly delicious, house-made, whole-food confections. Inspired by a raw "cheesecake" I tried there, these bars, with neat layers of tahini and berry cream, are so silky, so creamy, you'd never know they're dairy-free. Thanks, cashews and coconut milk! Creating the layers does require multiple rounds of setting in the freezer, so these bars are best made on a lazy day at home. They're perfect for summer, when the berries are ripe, it's too hot to turn on the oven, and you're craving something light, cold, and just sweet enough.

(CONTINUED →)

Makes 15 small bars

FOR THE CRUST:

3 tablespoons coconut oil, plus more
  for greasing the pan

1 cup raw unsalted almonds

12 pitted dates

½ cup unsweetened coconut chips

½ teaspoon salt

FOR THE FILLINGS:

2½ cups raw cashews, soaked in
  boiling water for at least 2 hours
  and up to overnight

¾ cup full-fat coconut milk

⅓ cup plus 1 tablespoon real
  maple syrup

¼ cup coconut oil

2 tablespoons freshly squeezed lemon
  or lime juice

1 tablespoon vanilla extract

1 heaping cup chopped fresh
  strawberries or raspberries

⅓ cup freeze-dried strawberries

¼ cup tahini

FOR THE TOPPING:

3 ounces dark chocolate,
  roughly chopped

2 tablespoons tahini

1½ teaspoons coconut oil

Flaky salt, for sprinkling

ı Line the bottom and sides of an 8-by-8-inch baking dish with parchment paper
  and grease with coconut oil or nonstick cooking spray.

2 To make the crust, in a food processor, blend the almonds, dates, coconut
  chips, coconut oil, and salt until it's sandy and sticky. It's okay if there are small
  bits of date remaining. Take care not to overprocess into nut butter! Press the
  crust into the bottom of the prepared pan with your fingers, then use the
  bottom of a measuring cup or a glass to press it down evenly. Pop the pan into
  the freezer.

CONTINUED→

3   To make both fillings, rinse the food processor bowl or grab a blender and add the drained cashews, coconut milk, maple syrup, coconut oil, citrus juice, and vanilla and blend until ethereally smooth and creamy, about the consistency of pudding. Scoop half of the filling (about 1½ cups) into a bowl and set aside.

4   Add the fresh and freeze-dried berries to the food processor or blender with the remaining half of the filling and blend until completely smooth, with no bits remaining. Transfer the berry filling to a container with a lid and refrigerate.

5   Stir the tahini into the bowl of remaining filling until completely incorporated. Spread the tahini cream evenly over the crust. Put the pan back into the freezer for about an hour, or until the tahini layer is firm.

6   Evenly spread the berry filling on top of the frozen tahini layer and freeze until completely firm, at least 1 hour.

7   To make the topping, melt the chocolate, tahini, and coconut oil in a double boiler (a glass bowl that fits into a pot, hovering over a few inches of boiling water, works great) or microwave, stirring frequently until melted and smooth.

8   Lift the bars out of the baking dish using the corners of the parchment paper and cut them into 1.5-by-3-inch rectangles. Place the bars on a cooling rack fitted over a baking sheet or cutting board and spoon the melted chocolate on top of each bar, spreading evenly using the back of a teaspoon and letting some drip over the edges, being sure not to completely cover up your beautiful layers. Sprinkle each bar with a little flaky salt. Freeze for about 15 minutes, or until the chocolate hardens.

9   Store the bars in the fridge in an airtight container if you plan to eat them within a day. Otherwise, store them in the freezer and let them soften up for about 10 torturous minutes on the counter before eating. They'll keep in the freezer for a few weeks.

TAHINI BANOFFEE PIE

Before I met *Top Chef* judge Gail Simmons, I had never heard of banoffee pie, a portmanteau of banana + toffee. Gail was a guest on my podcast, *Your Last Meal*, and this ubiquitous British dessert is her absolute favorite, the sweet finale of her fantasy last meal. In this book of whisper-sweet desserts, banoffee stands out as the stickiest and sweetest, brought back into balance with a salty peanut-and-pretzel topping and unsweetened whipped cream. Making the toffee is an actual magic trick: a long, hot bath transforms a can of condensed milk into a luscious mahogany dulce de leche. But this magic takes time; start this step early or consider making the dulce the day before. This bake-free recipe is based on Gail's, from her excellent cookbook *Bringing It Home*.

Makes one 9½-inch pie

FOR THE DULCE DE LECHE:
1 (14-ounce) can sweetened
   condensed milk

FOR THE PIE:
1 stick (½ cup) salted butter, melted,
   plus more for greasing the pan
10 ounces chocolate cookies, such as
   chocolate Teddy Grahams
¾ cup tahini
3 medium bananas, sliced into
   ½-inch coins

2 cups heavy cream
¼ cup roasted, salted peanuts,
   roughly chopped
A handful of pretzels, crushed into
   small pieces, for garnish

CONTINUED →

1   To make the dulce de leche, remove the label from the can of condensed milk and wrap the can in tin foil so the glue doesn't gum up your pot.

2   **If using a stovetop:** Place the can on the bottom of a large pot and fill with water. The water level should be at least 5 inches above the can. Bring the water to a boil, then turn the heat down to low and cover the pot, making sure it continues to simmer for 3 hours. Check the pot frequently and add more water if the level dips. If the can isn't covered with water, it can explode. Using tongs, carefully remove the hot can and let it sit on the counter until completely cool. This could take several hours but will prevent hot caramel from exploding out of the can!

3   **If using an Instant Pot:** Place the metal trivet on the bottom of the pot and place the can on the trivet, resting on its side. Fill with water to the max fill line. It's very important the can is completely covered with water. Cook on high pressure for 22 minutes. Release the pressure and, using tongs, carefully remove the can and let it sit on the counter until completely cool. This could take several hours but will prevent the hot caramel from exploding out of the can!

4   To make the pie, grease a 9½-inch pie pan with butter or nonstick cooking spray.

5   In a food processor, blend the chocolate cookies until they're sandy crumbs. Stir in the melted butter.

6   Press the chocolate crust onto the bottom and up the sides of the pan using the bottom of a small glass. Refrigerate until firm, about 30 minutes.

7   Meanwhile, pour the cooled can of dulce de leche into a medium bowl and mix in the tahini.

 CONTINUED →

8   Spread the tahini dulce de leche over the crust (an offset spatula is helpful). Arrange the sliced bananas in overlapping circles over the dulce de leche; it may form two layers.

9   Using a hand mixer, stand mixer, or a good-fashioned whisk and elbow grease, beat the heavy cream until it just holds stiff peaks. Spoon the whipped cream on top, covering the entire pie with a thick, fluffy cloud. Refrigerate until chilled, 15 minutes to an hour before serving. Sprinkle the peanuts and pretzels on top just before serving. Store leftovers in the fridge, covered, for up to 3 days.

SUPER SESAME
ICE CREAM SUNDAES

As much as I love a floofy dessert or a slice of summer fruit pie, my all-time favorite sweet treat is a hot fudge sundae with whipped cream, nuts, and a cherry, or, better yet, an old-fashioned banana split. When I realized I had recipes for tahini whipped cream, chocolate tahini magic shell, and sesame brittle in the book, it felt obvious to bring them all together for a wholesome, Americana ice cream social. The tahini brings a bit of complexity and nuttiness to these classic ice cream toppings, but it's subtle enough you won't feel smacked in the face with sesame. Not that there's anything wrong with that!

Makes 4 bowls

2 pints of your favorite ice cream (or a 48-ounce tub, with leftovers)

2 bananas, sliced in half and then lengthwise

1 batch Chocolate Tahini Magic Shell (page 128)

Flaky salt, for sprinkling (optional)

1 batch Tahini Whipped Cream (page 113)

Chopped nuts, such as roasted, salted peanuts, almonds, or toasted walnuts, for sprinkling

Maraschino cherries, for topping

1 batch Crisp Sesame Seed Brittle (page 134), broken into shards

· Scoop the ice cream into four bowls, add a couple banana chunks to each, drizzle with the chocolate tahini magic shell, and sprinkle a little flaky salt on top before it sets. Spoon on a few dollops of tahini whipped cream, a sprinkle of nuts, and top each sundae with an iconic red cherry and a shard of crisp sesame seed brittle.

 CONTINUED

Chocolate Tahini Magic Shell

The secret to making magic shell is simple: coconut oil! If made in the microwave, this glossy, tahini-kissed chocolate sauce comes together in under two minutes. Pour it over your favorite ice cream (I love it with strawberry), get a little bougie with a sprinkle of flaky salt, and patiently wait about a minute for the chocolate to firm up.

Makes 1 cup

½ cup dark or semisweet chocolate chips (or 3.5 ounces of chopped dark chocolate)

½ cup tahini

¼ cup coconut oil (use refined if you don't want any coconut flavor)

¼ teaspoon salt

1 **If using the microwave:** Put all the ingredients into a microwave-safe bowl and heat for 30-second increments until smooth and melted, 1 to 1½ minutes. Stir vigorously every 30 seconds to help the melting process.

2 **If using a stovetop:** Add a few inches of water to a small pot and fit a small glass or metal bowl over it. The bowl shouldn't touch the water. Heat the water to a gentle boil, add all the ingredients to the bowl, turn down the heat, and gently melt the chocolate, stirring frequently.

3 Let the sauce cool down from hot to warm before drizzling over ice cream. Store leftovers in a sealed container in a cool, dry place—not the refrigerator. No need to reheat—leftover magic shell can be poured over ice cream at room temperature.

GOAT CHEESE, HONEY, AND TAHINI
CHEESECAKE

I never had a homemade birthday cake growing up. Brownies came from a box mix and the Girl Scouts did most of the cookie baking. But my mom had one dessert in her repertoire, an excellent cheesecake topped with a layer of sweetened sour cream and a kaleidoscope of sliced kiwi. When I asked her for the recipe, she produced a yellowed, spiral bound, typewritten cookbook compiled by my dad's colleagues in the 1980s. I made the recipe my own, swapping in tangy goat cheese, honey, crushed pistachios, and tahini, a sumptuous Mediterranean feast best suited for a tangle of lounging, gossiping golden goddesses. This cheesecake is impossibly silky, far less dense than its New York cousin, and comes out creamy and custardy without the fuss of a springform pan or a water bath.

Makes one 9½-inch cake

FOR THE CRUST:

7 graham crackers

⅓ cup unsalted pistachios

2 tablespoons toasted sesame seeds

2 tablespoons sugar

6 tablespoons salted butter, melted

FOR THE FILLING:

1 (8-ounce) package of cream cheese

1 (4-ounce) tube of goat cheese

¼ cup plus 2 tablespoons honey

2 large eggs

1 teaspoon vanilla extract

¼ cup tahini

FOR THE TOPPING:

1 cup sour cream

2 tablespoons honey

1 teaspoon tahini

1 Preheat the oven to 350 degrees F.

2 To make the crust, pulverize the graham crackers to a fine crumb, either in a food processor or with a rolling pin in a ziplock bag. Add the pistachios and lightly blitz or crush so there are still small bits remaining. Stir in the sesame seeds and sugar. Add the butter and mix with a spatula until everything is uniformly saturated.

3 Press the graham cracker mixture into a 9½-inch pie pan using the bottom of a small glass or jar, pushing the crumbs up the sides to form a crust. Bake the crust for 12 to 15 minutes, on the center rack, until it's a shade darker than golden brown.

4 While the crust bakes, make the filling. In a stand mixer or in a medium bowl with an electric hand mixer, beat the cream cheese, goat cheese, and honey on medium high speed until fluffy and there are no cheese clumps remaining. Scrape down the sides of the bowl, add the eggs and vanilla, and mix until they're incorporated. Scrape down the bowl again, add the tahini, and beat until silky smooth.

5 Pour the filling into the pie crust and bake for 20 minutes. The center of the pie will still be jiggly, but the top shouldn't be wet.

6 While the filling bakes, make the topping. Mix the sour cream with the honey and tahini in a small bowl, making sure all the honey is incorporated.

7 Pull out the pie and gently dollop the sour cream topping all over the top of the filling. Use an offset spatula or a rubber spatula to gently and evenly smooth it over the filling. Bake for another 10 minutes.

8 Pull the pie from the oven and let it cool on the counter for 10 minutes before transferring it to the fridge (you might want to set it on a pot holder or wire rack). Let it chill in the fridge for at least 5 hours or overnight.

9 Store leftovers in the fridge, covered, for up to 4 days.

BLACK SESAME DATE SHOOTHIE

You've heard of *Ugly Delicious*? Well, this frothy treat is . . . Gloomy Delicious™! Glossy and inky, black sesame paste not only adds toasty, earthy flavor, it also blends up into a goth-approved potion the color of brooding gray storm clouds. Not quite a breakfast smoothie, but not exactly a shake, I veered into Bennifer portmanteau territory and a shoothie was born. While you *could* blend one up in the morning, I love to pour myself a nice tall glass of storm clouds in the afternoon when, like clockwork, my sweet tooth comes a-knockin' but I don't want to sugar crash. Black sesame paste is available at well-stocked Asian markets, specialty food shops, or online.

Makes two 8-ounce cups or one 16-ounce glass

½ medium banana

½ cup whole milk or alternative milk (something creamy, not nonfat)

4 to 6 plump pitted dates (depending on their size)

¼ cup pure unsweetened black sesame paste

8 ice cubes

Pinch of salt

- Add everything to a blender in the order listed, starting with 4 dates, and blend until completely smooth and frothy. If you'd like it sweeter, add another date. If you'd like it colder, use a frozen banana.

CRISP SESAME SEED BRITTLE

If you're a fan of sesame crunch candy—those tiny bricks of sweet, sticky sesame seeds wrapped in clear plastic—you're going to love this snappy, buttery brittle. This recipe is quick and easy, and you probably have all the ingredients in your pantry. Break off a rustic shard to garnish a scoop of ice cream (like in my Super Sesame Ice Cream Sundaes on page 127) or snack on it while standing barefoot at your kitchen counter.

Makes 1 foot-long sheet

¼ cup toasted white sesame seeds

2 tablespoons black sesame seeds (or you can also use all white)

¼ cup sugar

1½ tablespoons unsalted butter, cut into pieces

Pinch of salt

1   Prepare two 15-by-13-inch sheets of parchment paper, or one silicone baking mat and one sheet of parchment.

2   Heat a small pan over medium high and add the sugar, butter, and salt. Turn the heat down to medium or medium low if it's cooking too quickly, and stir constantly with a rubber spatula until it melts into a smooth, light caramel color. Turn off the heat, add the sesame seeds, and mix until fully incorporated.

NOTE: If your sesame seeds aren't toasted, add them to a dry pan and toast over medium heat until lightly golden, stirring and watching constantly so they don't get too dark.

3   Pour the sesame caramel onto the center of one sheet of parchment or a silicone mat, cover with the other piece of parchment, and use a rolling pin to spread it into a ⅛-inch-thick sheet.

4   Let it completely cool, 15 to 20 minutes, peel off the parchment, and break into whatever size pieces you'd like. Store leftover brittle in a sealed container at room temperature for up to a week.

Sorry
OSED
SESAME

ACKNOWLEDGMENTS

I have wanted to write a book since I was five years old, and creating this one was one of the great joys of my life. But I couldn't have done it alone. I have been looking forward to thanking all the people I love and appreciate in permanent ink!

Thanks to Jen Worick, publisher at Sasquatch Books, for inviting me to write *Open Sesame*. I am so grateful for the opportunity, for your friendship, and, oh jeez, I'm tearing up right meow! To my editor Jill Saginario, you made this process so easy and fun, gave me permission to be myself, and have been so encouraging, calm, positive, and helpful at every turn. Thanks to Charity Burggraaf, Tony Ong, and Alison Keefe for making this book so beautiful! I couldn't ask for a more talented, creative, and sweet team!

So much gratitude for my recipe testers, who consistently impressed me with their type A attention to detail and thoughtful notes. You helped make these recipes better *and* you are some of my favorite people: Carrie Stradley, Diane Duthweiler, Genevieve Haas, Jack Volpi, Minh-Hai Alex, Mindy Jennings, Natalie Berglund, Noelle Nightengale, Renee McMahon, Ron Upshaw, Sandy Lam, Sue Mills, and Yoko Feinman.

To my Super Testers, who eagerly and generously volunteered to do extra credit: Simone Alger, my oldest friend and superstar baker buddy, I will now make *you* sit on the bath mat while I read this entire cookbook to you from my toilet throne! Dearest friends Kennedy Soileau, my partner in pun, and

Andrea O'Meara, please move back to Seattle this instant, young lady! Much love to my right-hand gal, Jess Aceti, the most generous friend who gives the best advice and makes the best salad dressings. How many camels?

Thanks to Jill Lightner for your front porch advice and to Maleeha Syed for your cute hands.

A big hug for Isaac Mizrahi, one of the funniest food-loving folks. Thank you for your support and generosity—we should definitely have a child together!

Love to Bryan Mills for your constant encouragement, generosity, friendship, and adventure kinship. You're the spaghetti in my cal-zone-ee. Thanks for getting your hooves shined up for the shoot! Love to Cathy Tuttle for always being my #1 cheerleader, even when I morph into my evil alter ego, Snobby McFoodiePants.

Is . . . is this where one would thank a cat? I LOVE YOU, POPPO, YOU'RE GORGEOUS! Thank you to my parents for raising me as an adventurous eater and for encouraging and supporting my creativity.

To everyone who listens to my podcast, *Your Last Meal*, and who listened to me on Seattle radio for so many years, your support and enthusiasm for my work helped make this cookbook possible—thank you!

INDEX

PHOTO BY SANDY LAM

ABOUT THE AUTHOR

RACHEL BELLE is the creator and host of the podcast *Your Last Meal*, a James Beard Award finalist, and host of *The Nosh with Rachel Belle*, a food-themed TV show on Seattle's Cascade PBS. She spent twenty years as a broadcast journalist, winning the national Edward R. Murrow Award for news radio feature reporting; was named Seattle's Best FM Radio Personality by *Seattle Weekly*; and did a bunch of food writing for many publications that no longer exist (loved you, *Lucky Peach*!). Rachel is an enthusiastic home cook and cookbook recipe tester who especially loves cooking in camper-vans and over campfires. She doesn't believe in blueberry bagels and lives in Seattle, Washington.

Copyright © 2024 by Rachel Belle

All rights reserved. No portion of this book may be reproduced or utilized in any form, or by any electronic, mechanical, or other means, without the prior written permission of the publisher.

Printed in China

SASQUATCH BOOKS with colophon is a registered trademark of Penguin Random House LLC

28 27 26 25 24   9 8 7 6 5 4 3 2 1

Editor: Jill Saginario
Production editor: Isabella Hardie
Photographs and styling: Charity Burggraaf
Designer: Tony Ong

Page xiv photo by Bryan Mills, styling assistance and direction by Jessica Aceti, photo editing by Brian Kirk and Jessica Aceti

Library of Congress Cataloging-in-Publication Data
Names: Belle, Rachel, author.
Title: Open sesame : 45 sweet and savory recipes for tahini & all things sesame / Rachel Belle.
Description: Seattle : Sasquatch Books, [2024]
Identifiers: LCCN 2024009813 | ISBN 9781632175274 (paperback) | ISBN 9781632175281 (ebook)
Subjects: LCSH: Cooking (Tahini) | Sesame. | LCGFT: Cookbooks.
Classification: LCC TX814.5.S47 B45 2024 | DDC 641.6/385--dc23/eng/20240312
LC record available at https://lccn.loc.gov/2024009813

The recipes contained in this book have been created for the ingredients and techniques indicated. Neither publisher nor author is responsible for your specific health or allergy needs that may require supervision. Nor are publisher and author responsible for any adverse reactions you may have to the recipes contained in the book, whether you follow them as written or modify them to suit your personal dietary needs or tastes.

ISBN: 978-1-63217-527-4

Sasquatch Books
1325 Fourth Avenue, Suite 1025
Seattle, WA 98101

SasquatchBooks.com

MIX
Paper | Supporting responsible forestry
FSC
www.fsc.org
FSC® C008047